The Anchor of Our Purest Thoughts (Book 4)

THE TALE OF TWO MINDS

The Art and Science of
Decision-making in
Everyday Life

DR. CHONG CHEN

Brain & Life Publishing
London

ISBN 978-1-912533-03-9 Paperback

Brain & Life Publishing

27 Old Gloucester Street, London, U.K.

First Printing, 2018

For information about special needs for bulk purchases, sales promotions, and educational needs, please contact orders@brainandlife.net.

The Anchor of Our Purest Thoughts Series

1. *Fitness Powered Brains: Optimize Your Productivity, Leadership and Performance*

2. *Chocolate and the Nobel Prize: The Book of Brain Food*

3. *Cleverland: The Science of How Nature Nurtures*

4. *The Tale of Two Minds: The Art and Science of Decision-making in Everyday Life*

5. *Strategic Memory: The Natural History of Learning and Forgetting*

To Arisa and my parents for their love and support

Table of Contents

Preface

I did not know the world of cats and dogs differs from ours. Theirs is not so colorful. They cannot see all the colors we see because their eyes don't have all of the special light catching cells we have. The same world, but a different color to cats, dogs, and us, which begs the question, what is the real color of the world?

Unfortunately, it seems we will never get the answer. Nobody knows the real color of the world, as we are limited by our vision. Cats and dogs can't see the rainbow as we see it because the color spectrum of the rainbow goes beyond their eyes. Similarly, we can't see the world as it is because the real color of the world may go beyond our eyes.

In fact, not only our physical eyes, the eye of our heart or mind, or the so-called mind's eye, also has its limitation. We all interpret the world with our own mindset, deviating from reality. Okay, dear reader, don't worry. I won't go pessimistic. I just want to point out that we are constrained by our mindset and the moment we think beyond our old mindset, it will be a revolutionary experience.

In his classic *The Structure of Scientific Revolutions*, philosopher Thomas S. Kuhn famously argued that scientific revolutions are paradigm shifts. Ultimately, paradigm means a theoretical structure, a mindset, a worldview, and a pair of eyes. A scientific revolution gives us a new pair of eyes. The world is still the same world, but the eyes through which we see the world change.

The impact of acquiring a pair of new eyes is remarkable. To vividly experience such impact, here is an example. Please spend several minutes considering this problem.

A devout monk is going to worship Buddha in a temple on the top of a mountain. In the morning, when the sun just appears on the horizon, he begins to climb from the foot of the mountain. The mountain is high, and there is only one curving road to the top. Until the sun is about to go down, the monk finally arrives at the temple. The monk prays in the evening, and the next morning, when the sun just appears on the horizon, he begins to go downhill. So, is it possible for the monk to pass the same place on the road at the same time on these two days?

From the content of the story, we can easily infer that the monk goes down faster than up, so for the same period of time, he walks down the mountain longer in distance than up the mountain, he should reach the foot of the mountain before the sunset. But how can we infer if he is likely to pass the same place at the same time on those two days? Based on the reasoning above, we can't solve the problem.

Now, let us change our mindset. Instead of thinking about the above problem, think about another question: there are two monks going to worship. On the same morning at the time of sunrise, one goes up the mountain from the foot and the other goes down from the summit. Will they meet somewhere in the middle of the road?

At this moment, the answer instantly appears in our minds: they will. This clarity is in sharp contrast to the initial confusion born from considering the first question. This is the power of new eyes.

In this book, I want to share another paradigm of thinking that brings us new eyes: we have two minds, or two ways of thinking, reflective and intuitive. Reflective thinking or reflection is based on logic and analysis.

Intuitive thinking or intuition, on the other hand, is a non-reflective, gut feeling based on our past experiences.

If we look closely at hundreds, even thousands, of choices and decisions we make every day, we will find that most are based on the intuitive mind. I am not saying we are irrational or behaving sub-optimally, but realizing this fact will help us initiate a series of actions that improve our intuition because there is good and trustworthy intuition and there is bad and biased intuition. Cultivating the good and trustworthy and correcting the bad and biased is where reflection contributes its value.

The stories and studies introduced in this book have given me a pair of new eyes and helped me make decisions in everyday life. I am sure they will do the same thing for you. Good luck.

Chapter 1. Reflection and Intuition

We know more than we can tell.

— Michael Polanyi,
The Tacit Dimension (1966)

A bungalow in a residential area was on fire. The source of the fire appeared to be in the kitchen. Firefighters quickly entered the living room, set up a hose and began sprinkling water towards the kitchen. But the fire could not be controlled. It became even more intense. At this moment, the firefighters suddenly heard their chief shouting: "Get out of here NOW!" Just as the firefighters ran out of the house, the living room—where they just stood—collapsed!

Afterwards, upon reflection, the chief realized that the fire in the kitchen had been surprisingly quiet; the living room where they stood was unusually hot, and they did not get expected outcomes with spraying water towards the kitchen. This made him "feel strange." Although at the time when he shouted out "Get out of here NOW!" he did not know exactly what was strange. It turned out that the source of the fire was not in the kitchen. It was below the living room where the firefighters stood: the basement. However, at that time, the firefighters and the chief did not know that bungalow had a basement.

This was a true story told by Gary Klein, a U.S. decision-making psychologist, in his 1998 book *Sources of Power: How People Make Decisions*. Without knowing the reasons, the chief felt "strange." At the moment he shouted out, he could not explain exactly what was going on, but he was sure something was strange. How can we explain this feeling and where does it come from?

We know more than we can explain

Antonio Damasio, a neuroscientist at the University of Southern California, designed the *Iowa Gambling Task*. This is a laboratory game used to simulate decision-making in real life. In this task, people initially have the same amount of money to gamble with and make a profit. They must select a series of 100 cards from four decks, A, B, C, and D. They can select one card at a time and each card corresponds to either a win or loss.

What people do not know is two of the decks A and B are disadvantageous decks. Although the cards from these two decks are more profitable (such as $100), they are occasionally accompanied by large losses (hundreds or thousands of dollars). The more cards drawn from these two decks, the greater the net loss. The other two decks, C and D, are the advantageous decks. Although the payouts from these two decks are relatively small (such as $50), the occasional loss accompanied is also minimal (tens or hundreds of dollars). Drawing cards from decks C and D will eventually bring net gain.

As people gambled, Damasio monitored their physiological responses. He found that before people became subjectively aware of the advantageous and disadvantageous decks, their body already had generated an alarm signal. Usually, around the 10th card they selected, people had an anticipatory skin conductance response (SCR) to the bad decks. Their palms sweated whenever they wanted to withdraw a card from the bad decks. This was a physiological marker indicating the degree of emotional arousal.

Typically, under situations that induce fear, anger, or sexual arousal, the activity of the sympathetic nervous system increases and the sweat glands become more active. As a result, the palms sweat, the body chills, or the skin goose bumps. Lie detectors work based on this mechanism. Although people had a SCR, at this time they had no subjective consciousness concerning what happened.

Around the 50th and 60th cards, people had a gut feeling that decks A and B were the disadvantageous cards. They started to avoid decks A and B based on this feeling without knowing why. Around the time of the 80th card, people finally realized the reason. Although decks A and B produced large gains, their occasional losses were greater and they would have a net loss eventually. However, decks C and D, although they had small returns, their occasional losses were also small, and the net outcome was gain.

This feeling reported by subjects in the *Iowa Gambling Task* is actually the same thing as the "feel strange" sensation by the fire chief. These are just two examples of intuition we all have in our daily lives. Because people do not understand the process of how intuition is produced, people often refer to these feelings as magical "revelations," "foreboding," "the sixth sense," or "instincts." So, how does intuition come about? What is its source? To answer these questions, let us first look at the research paradigm of the mind.

The scientific study of the mind

On September 10th, 1956, a group of leading psychologists, linguists, and computer scientists gathered at the Massachusetts Institute of Technology to hold a three-day academic conference. The theme of the conference was "Information Theory." On the second day of the meeting, computer scientist Allen Newell and Herbert Simon from Carnegie Mellon University presented a paper entitled "Logic Theory Machine," MIT linguist Noam Chomsky presented "Three Models for the Description of Language," and George Miller, the Harvard psychologist, presented "The Magic Number Seven."

Behind these three reports, there was a common concept that like a computer, the human brain thinks in a way similar to computing or information processing. This common concept is at the intersection of psychology, linguistics, and computer science. The new paradigm of information processing made this conference—and this day, September 11th, 1956—the beginning of the "cognitive revolution" in scientific psychology and the birth of "cognitive science."

According to this new paradigm, the process of our mind or thinking is considered the computer information processing system. In simple terms, this system is divided into three parts or steps: input, processing, and output. Input is raw materials, processing computation or manipulation, and output the result of computation.

Based on this paradigm, Stanford psychologist Richard Atkinson and his student Richard Shiffrin proposed a model in 1968 that dissected the process of memory.

As shown in Figure 1, people first attend to and perceive information in the external environment through five senses to generate a "sensory register," which is also called "sensory memories." Whereas some sensory memories are forgotten and lost, some can be stored in the brain for a short period and are called "short-term memories." Depending on the importance of such information or whether people repeat it or not, short-term memory is further stored in "long-term memory" or forgotten.

External Environment

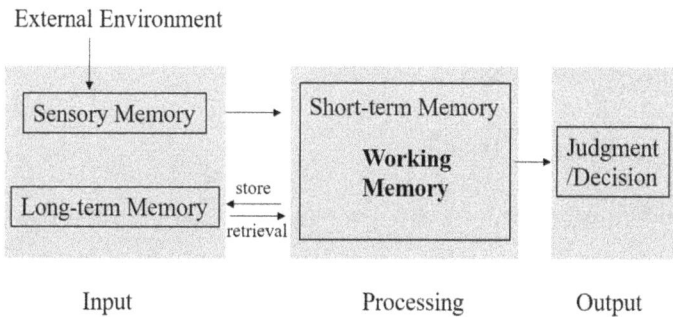

| Input | Processing | Output |

Figure 1. The process model of memory

Short-term memory currently active and being manipulated in the brain—meaning they come from sensory memory or are retrieved from long-term memory—is also known as working memory. Although strictly speaking, short-term memory and working memory are two different concepts used in distinct contexts, here for the purpose of simplicity, we treat them as the same.

Working memory contains all the raw materials that the brain uses for processing. Interestingly, it was recently discovered that only part of working memory is available to the subjective consciousness. In fact, consciousness is a subset of working memory. The brain processes working memory following certain rules and then obtains the output of the information processing: a specific judgment or decision.

Intuition revisited

Therefore, from the perspective of information processing, the characteristic nature of intuition is that we only know the output of information processing and are not clear about what the raw material is and how that material is processed (see Table 1).

Thus, the fire chief only knew the output of information processing "feel strange" and "get out of here NOW." Some of the raw material was recalled only afterward: the surprisingly quiet fire in the kitchen, the unusually hot floor of the living room, and the unsuccessful effort of spraying water towards the kitchen. Even afterward, he knew nothing about the procedure of the information processing: how his mind reached those conclusions that saved their lives. Similarly, at the beginning of the *Iowa Gambling Task*, people only had sweaty palms and some gut feelings towards the bad decks; they did not know the reason why.

Table 1. Differentiating reflection and intuition from the paradigm of information processing.
(√ consciously aware; ? consciously unaware)

	Intuition	Reflection
Input	?	√
Processing	?	√
Output	√	√

In everyday life, intuition looks like a mysterious revelation, a sixth sense. Intuition seems mysterious simply because people subjectively know nothing about its early stages (input and processing). To put it another way, this early stage is a "subconscious" or "unconscious" phenomenon of information processing that the conscious does not recognize.

With unconsciousness, I think it is necessary to clarify what that means. Unconsciousness is the mental world we do not know with our subjective consciousness. The popularization of unconsciousness is largely attributed to the Austrian psychoanalyst Sigmund Freud. Freud believed that we know only a tiny part of our psychological world, especially the emotional world, as most of it is unconscious. If we treat our mind as a floating iceberg, then consciousness is only the small part above the surface of the water, while unconsciousness is the larger part that hides below the water.

The notion of unconsciousness is true and has stood the test of scientific psychology and neuroscience. But that does not mean Freud's interpretation of unconsciousness is correct. In his psychoanalytic theory, Freud regarded unconsciousness as the contradiction and impulse of "sex" and "anger" suppressed by people's subjective consciousness because they are not accepted by reality and morality. Essentially, the unconsciousness is barbaric and evil. Freud's interpretation was with no empirical evidence and much of his theory proved wrong.

Nowadays, the unconsciousness accepted by the scientific community is another "good" unconsciousness. It is an efficient and adaptive information processing mechanism formed in the process of human evolution and individual learning. Social psychologist Timothy D. Wilson at the University of Virginia calls it "the adaptive unconscious." This adaptive unconsciousness is the basis of intuition and affects our judgment and decision-making in everyday life.

Two minds

So we have two thinking systems or two minds. Differently put, our judgment and decision-making process consists of two parallel information processing modes: one where we subjectively only know of the output but not the input and procedure of information processing, is intuition; the other, in which we are aware of the input, procedure, and output of information processing, is reflection.

Psychologists have given many names to these two modes of thinking. For instance, intuition is also called System 1, the experiential system, the associative system, the hot system, heuristic processing, intuitive cognition, and automatic process. Reflection is referred to as System 2, the analytical system, the rule-based system, the cold system, systematic processing, analytical cognition, and controlled process.

Reflection is the mode during which we use currently active information in our subjective consciousness (i.e., conscious working memory) to do logic reasoning or inference. We clearly know the input (conscious information in the working memory), the process (logic reasoning), and the output (conclusion, see Table 1).

It must be noted that the output of reflection is not necessarily logical or rational. Reflection is the process by which people deal with the information they receive and is based on the logic reasoning principles they have learned. To what extent people's conclusion from their reflection is rational depends on the quality of their obtained information (such as representativeness and accuracy) and their inference capacity (the principles of logical reasoning that one has learned and their general intelligence).

Intuition is unconscious, automatic, spontaneous information processing. The input may contain not only conscious information currently active in working memory, but also unconscious information in working memory. The unconscious information in working memory is from sensory memory (environmental cues perceived by the sensory organs) and long-term memory (stored experience). The operation of information is generally associative: starting from one thing and automatically linking to other things. The process is unconscious and largely influenced by emotions.

We do not understand the raw materials and the specific process of intuition. Intuition usually tells us the result of its operation in the form of feelings. As we discussed earlier, unconsciousness is not the evil, suppressed unconscious popularized by Freud, but rather an efficient and adaptive information processing mode that has evolved in the course of human evolution and individual learning.

Reflection requires many mental resources and much effort as it runs slowly. Intuition consumes less or no effort and runs fast. The two modes of information processing are not independent, but influences the other. Intuition often automatically provides its conclusions to reflection, whereas reflection can follow or correct intuitive conclusions. Now, let us look deeper at the concepts of the two minds.

The reflective mind

The input or raw material for reflection is the active information in our subjective consciousness, primarily language, symbols, and numbers. The process of information processing is logical reasoning, including mathematical calculation.

In the *Iowa Gambling Task*, the choices people made after identifying the two disadvantageous decks were reflective thinking. Faced with two decks of cards with large rewards but even larger losses, and two decks with small rewards but also smaller losses (input), people can simply do the math (processing) and conclude the decks with net gain are better than those with net loss (output). They accordingly draw cards from the two advantageous decks.

Psychologists define this process as "problem solving," and think rational problem solving should include the following steps:

1. Define and specify the problem: clarify and understand the problem by collecting as much information as possible;

2. Identify obstacles and available resources, and set realistic goals of decision-making, such as the maximization of profits;

3. Think of a variety of solutions: under the guidance of the decision-making goals, find out as many alternative options as possible, including action plans;

4. Compare various solutions: judge and compare the possible pros and cons of various solutions according to the goals;

5. Choose the solution: the best or most effective one;

6. Implement the solution: carry out the solution and corresponding action plan;

7. Evaluate the decision: seek feedback and evaluate the quality of decision-making.

Economists use "utility" as the criterion of profit. Utility is a personal preference that depends on people's values, including their motives and goals. To reflect and decide, one first must clearly understand one's own values. When comparing various solutions or options, the "expected utility" of each solution is first calculated by using the dimension-weighted strategy, that is, the weighted sum of all the utilities that a solution can bring multiplied by the probability of each utility. The one with the greatest expected utility is the best solution. Economists believe this strategy is what rational people (an "economic man") should use.

Therefore, to make rational decisions, we must first think of many alternative options, weigh the pros and cons, and choose the optimal one. A classic example of weighing the pros and cons of an option was used by 18th-century American politician and scientist Benjamin Franklin:

"My way is to divide half a sheet of paper by a line into two columns; writing over the one Pro and over the other Con. Then during three or four days' consideration, I put down under the different heads short hints of the different motives, that at different time occur to me, for or against the measure. When I have thus got them altogether in one view, I endeavor to estimate their respective weights; and where I find two, one on each side, that seem equal, I strike them both out. If I judge some two reasons con equal to some three reasons pro, I strike out five; and thus proceeding, I find where the balance lies; and if after a day or two of further consideration, nothing new that is of importance occurs on either side, I come to a determination accordingly. And though the weight of reasons cannot be taken with the precision of algebraic quantities, yet when each is thus considered separately and comparatively, and the whole lies before me, I think I can judge better, and am less likely to make a rash step; and in fact I have found great advantage from this kind

of equation, in what may be called moral or prudential algebra."

For Franklin to choose among a pool of options, he had to first weigh the pros and cons of each option separately, and then compare them.

Now, we know reflection is analytical, evidence-based, and logic-guided thinking. It consumes much effort. But it may bring us more profit in cases of problems that can be easily quantified. In everyday life, people tend to believe reflection is more important than intuition.

The intuitive mind

Intuition is a feeling we have. This feeling can be fluent, easily found hunches; it can also be sudden and abrupt "inspiration" or "insight." Its source of information and process of computation is unclear to us. All the information stored in our brain, whether or not we deliberately recall it, is the raw materials of intuition.

In a given situation, intuition is the product of the free association of knowledge and experience in our brain. The start of the free association is primarily the environment cues stored in the sensory memory and working memory. The end of the free association is the stored information in the long-term memory. In other words, the situation provides us cues, which we store in sensory memory and working memory; these cues further link to whatever related information we possess in our long-term memory. The outcome of the free association is intuition that occurs in our minds.

This mechanism can also help us understand why intuition can be right or wrong. The latter depends on the matching of our knowledge and experience with the situation. Long-term memory can produce accurate intuition only when there is a corresponding reserve of knowledge, which can adequately reflect the needs of the current situation.

Instead of following the steps of reflection, the fire chief came out with the intuitive conclusion of feeling "strange" and everyone should "Get out of here NOW!" This intuition was accurate because he unconsciously obtained all the necessary cues, and his long-term memory had a wealth of experience in firefighting. We will discuss in what situation intuition is correct, and in what situation it is not shortly, but for now let's talk about a special form of intuition.

Emotions: A special form of intuition

The emotion we talk about here is more strictly an emotional response or reaction. It refers to the emotional experience that an object, person, or event brings to us and is a subjective experience and feeling that depends on our values (including motives and goals).

When we get messages (positive feedback) consistent with our values from the environment, we have positive emotions such as happiness, proudness, gratitude, and love. Conversely, when we obtain information inconsistent with our values (negative feedback) from the environment, we have negative emotions such as sadness, anger, blame, and anxiety.

Emotional reactions are generally accompanied by cognitive evaluations (thoughts), physical body signs (facial expressions, heart rate, and changes in body hormones) and behavioral tendencies (fight or flight). Often after we obtain certain information, we can quickly, automatically, effortlessly, or even involuntarily produce a specific emotional response, as if there is no internal information processing needed. When emotional reactions occur, we have some kind of feelings, namely emotional experiences, immediately.

However, often, we do not know subjectively how these experiences are produced. We are not aware of the unconscious early stage of our emotional experiences. Therefore, emotional reactions are also intuition.

In the *Iowa Gambling Task*, before people figured out the truth in their consciousness, their reactions to the disadvantageous decks was just a bad emotional response (palms sweating) and a risky feeling. But it was this feeling that successfully guided them to avoid the disadvantageous decks. From this perspective, this automatic and rapid emotional response can help adapt to certain environments and cope with risks.

Chapter 2. Which Mind is Better?

If it was always optimal to follow our affective and experiential instincts, there would have been no need for the rational/ analytic system of thinking to have evolved and become so prominent in human affairs.

— Paul Slovic and Colleagues,
The Affect Heuristic (2002)

You can do an interesting experiment with your family and friends. When you walk with them, ask them to do a mental math problem, such as 32 X 57, and see if they can keep their walking pace. You will find they unconsciously slow down or even stop to calculate (unless they are proficient in math). A simple mental math problem has this effect, not to mention the impact of complicated discussions. As I walked with friends, we often talked about some academic issues. Each time we talked about a topic that required in-depth reflection, some of us would involuntarily stop, and the person's symbolic language was: "wait a moment."

Under normal circumstances, people talk intuitively while walking. We speak mostly about what springs to our mind and do not reflect deeply upon it. Without serious thinking, we can easily walk at a consistent, comfortable pace. Thinking of complex or important issues consumes a lot of mental resources and is constrained by our limited working memory. This will compete with the small part of the mental resource that normally controls walking. The result is we slow down, or stop all together.

It is easy to understand that when we go up and down the stairs, if we focus too much on thinking, reading a book, or playing games on a smartphone we suddenly step on a wrong step. This may also explain why depressive patients generally walk slower than non-depressed people do, because the former is constantly thinking about their own fault or misfortune.

It seems that we do not need complicated discussions and calculations: simple counting, such as from one to ten, can severely damage our performance on tasks that require working memory. In my own experiments in neuroscience, rat brain slices are made by inserting blades in sequence on the incisions 10, 14, 12, 16 of the slicing device. My colleagues and I often find that when one is somewhere in the middle of his counting from incision 1 to 10, once he is spoken to by another person he must restart his counting from the beginning. Why? He forgets what number he has counted to.

After hearing about our experiences, a friend brought up a similar scene in a comedy. In the laboratory, the female character let the male character help her count the number of bacterial spores on the dish through a microscope while she went out. When the male character counted to 367, the female character came back and asked him how the counting was going. The male character replied dismissively: "How's the counting going? When I was in kindergarten, I was able to recite pi back to 1000 after the decimal point for the school talent show. Can this counting thing bite me?" The female character said, "Great, go ahead." Then the male character began to look back into the microscope, and the audience heard him say, "Damn! 1, 2, 3..."

The magic number seven

Regarding our limited capacity for information processing in consciousness, as the Harvard psychologist George Miller reported at the 1956 MIT meeting that marked the birth of the cognitive revolution, our brains can hold or think about seven (plus or minus two, there is an individual difference) items at a time.

This is the maximal amount of information our brain can consciously handle. Miller called it the "magic number seven."

Try to remember this sequence of numbers:

83550104781

Hard?

We can consciously hold up to seven items in our mind, seven numbers, seven names, seven words, seven concepts, or seven sounds simultaneously. If we add more to our brain, we cannot remember. Unless they are grouped or categorized. For instance, if the above sequence of numbers is divided into three groups, it will be far easier to remember, 8355-010-4781. This is also the common way we remember and exchange phone numbers. This is called "chunking." But again, we can only handle up to seven groups, seven categories. A sequence like 8355-010-4781-6488-297-8946-6857-153-1875 is difficult to remember.

Later research has found that Miller's magic number seven may be an ideal maximization. The information that can be reliably stored in our consciousness or conscious working memory may be only 3 to 4, and sometimes no more than 2 items. This is particularly true when we solve problems and make decisions in daily life.

Roger N. Shepard, a former postdoc fellow of Miller and now a Professor Emeritus at Stanford University said,

"Possibly our feeling that we can take account of a host of different factors comes about because although we remember that at some time or other we have attended to each of the different factors, we fail to notice that it is seldom more than one or two that we consider at any one time."

The limited capacity of our conscious working memory is the main factor that constrains the efficiency of reflection. It is because of this limited working memory we have to restrain from any conversation when we count brain slices during the experiment. To get rid of the limitation of conscious working memory, when we count the number of cells under the microscope, we have been using manual counters. Whenever we see a cell, we click the counter and it automatically accumulates.

Fast, effortless first impressions

You visit a friend living in another city. One day, your friend is busy and you decide to go out and look around. By the way, you also help your friend return a few books to the city library. Although your friend told you where the library is, you still get lost. You decide to find someone and ask the way. At this time, you come across a boy wearing glasses and carrying a school bag. He walks fast. You guess perhaps he is a student and late for school. You decide not to bother him.

After the boy comes a pair of middle-aged couples who talk and laugh from moment to moment. They carry shopping bags, perhaps having just returned from the supermarket. They look kind, so you decide to ask them. They tell you the direction and the estimated distance.

On your way to the library, a bearded man stops you and says he lost this wallet, and whether you can kindly give him a little change to catch the bus. Although he looks insincere and you don't trust him, you give him a few bucks. After arriving at the library, a female librarian wearing glasses tells you, with a serious facial expression, that two of the books have expired. After you pay the fare and return to your friend's home, you tell your friend how you met an unfriendly person in the library today.

Like this, in everyday life, we make quick and effortless judgments on people we meet. What they look like, whether they are in a hurry, kind, sincere, or indifferent. So how accurate are these fast, effortless judgments?

To answer this question, Harvard psychologist Nalini Ambady recorded videos of college teachers delivering lectures. The teachers varied in their backgrounds, such as humanities, social sciences, and natural sciences. Ambady chose 10 seconds from the beginning, the middle, and the end of each teacher's lesson and turned off the sound. She then played the three 10-second silent videos to college students who had not seen the teachers before. The college students easily evaluated 15 traits about the effectiveness of the teaching, such as abilities, self-confidence, enthusiasm, liveliness, sincerity, popularity, and optimism.

Ambady then compared the ratings to those by students who had sat in the teachers' classes for an entire semester. Surprisingly, the correlation coefficient between them was 0.76. After statistically controlling the influence of the teachers' appearance (or attraction), the correlation coefficient was still as high as 0.74.

Ambedy further shortened all 3 videos to 2 seconds and found that students' ratings were nearly identical to those of three 10-second videos. The correlation coefficient of the new ratings with those by students who had sat in the teachers' classes for an entire semester was 0.71.

In statistics, a correlation coefficient of 0.71 means that two variables can interpret each other's variation by 50%. Variation reflects the extent to which individuals in a group differ from one another or from the average, and is used to make group comparisons. It can be inferred that a student unfamiliar with the professor, after viewing three 2-second lecturing videos, can rate his effectiveness as 50% accurate as the average student who has listened to the teacher for an entire semester. This is the power of our intuition in the formation of first impressions.

This is in sharp contrast to the earlier activities of doing mental math problems and counting, which are slow and laborious. The complex and sophisticated first impressions towards other people are formed quickly and effortlessly. That is because the former relies on reflection, whose information processing capability is limited; the latter relies on intuition, whose information processing capability is almost infinite.

The magic number 11,000,000

By counting the number of receptors and nerve fibers in our sensory organs, neuroscientists have estimated that the information we can process (both consciously and unconsciously) is about 11 million bits per second. As shown in Table 2, our eyes can process 10 million bits per second, skin 1 million, ears and nose 100,000 each, tongue 1000. We are taking in all of that information, but we are only aware of a fraction of it. The amount of information these organs can handle under consciousness is pitiful, the eyes 40 bits per second, skin 5, ears 30, nose 1, and tongue 1.

Table 2. The amount of information our sensory organs can handle per second (bits)

	Total amount	Under consciousness
Eyes	10 million	40
Skin	1 million	5
Ears	100,000	30
Nose	100,000	1
Tongue	1000	1

But even this tiny amount of sensory information, the reflective mind cannot handle well. Miller's magic number seven tells us that the reflective mind can hold 7 items at once, which is equivalent to 2.8 bits. It is negligible compared to the capacity of the unconscious.

Thanks to this enormous information processing power and the associative processing style, the capacity of the unconscious in integrating information is tremendous. Based on environmental cues, intuition associates and integrates with past experiences stored in long-term memory. This process is highly efficient and requires little effort.

A large amount of information is processed at the intuitive, unconscious level, and the results of such processing are provided to the conscious and reflection in the form of feelings. This process does not require the brain to experience its operation at the conscious level and hence is not limited by our conscious, working memory capacities.

Looking at strangers for seconds, their facial expressions, gestures, movements, and other information will be perceived by the unconscious (only part of them enter consciousness). People automatically make associations and classifications, which helps form quick impressions and evaluations.

In the *Iowa Gambling Task*, the winning and losing feedback from each card was well processed and synthesized in the unconscious to generate feelings of risk and danger. Before people consciously realized what was going on, they had already begun intuitively to avoid the risky, disadvantageous decks.

Similarly, the fire chief's sixth sense was fast. The fire scene, the sound of the fire burning, the temperature in the living room, and the outcome of spraying water towards the kitchen all registered in his unconsciousness.

The output of the unconscious processing, "feel strange" and "Get out of here NOW!" suddenly occurred to him and ultimately saved many lives. Only afterward did the chief understand what happened. If he spent a few more seconds to collect evidence and analyze the situation using his reflective mind, or if he did not trust his intuition, perhaps he and his colleagues would be on a memorial list.

The intuition in *Iowa Gambling Task* is an adaptive unconsciousness. The formation of first impressions of other people and the intuition of the fire chief are both expert intuition, which we will discuss in Chapter 3 and 4. But not all intuition have such advantages. Sometimes, the quick intuition is error-prone and biased.

Erroneous intuition

Now, quickly glance over the evaluation of your two new colleagues, A and B. Which one do you prefer?

A. smart—confident—tenacious—stubborn—arrogant—indifferent

B. indifferent—arrogant—stubborn—tenacious—confident—smart

If you are like most *Homo sapiens*, you instinctually prefer A. But if you compare them more closely, you will find that the descriptions of them are exactly the same, only the order of traits is reversed. Under the guidance of intuition, the initial information you received automatically creates in you certain expectations, which affects your processing of subsequent incoming information. This is known as the priming effect. The result is that you will naturally and confidently feel A is better than B.

This phenomenon reminds us of the critical role of our first impressions. At the same time, it reminds us of the deviant thinking that comes from our intuition. The automatic and rapid intuition helps us understand and categorize strangers as soon as possible, which is evolutionarily adaptive. However, sometimes, it also has to pay some prices.

Let us consider these three questions:

- A bat and a ball cost $1.10 in total. The bat costs $1.00 more than the ball. How much does the ball cost? _____ cents

- If it takes 5 machines 5 minutes to make 5 widgets, how long would it take 100 machines to make 100 widgets? _____ minutes

- In a lake, there is a patch of lily pads. Every day, the patch doubles in size. If it takes 48 days for the patch to cover the entire lake, how long would it take for the patch to cover half of the lake? _____ days

Dear reader be honest, did the answer of 10 cents, 100 minutes, and 24 days occur in your mind?

Managerial scientist Shane Frederick at MIT once asked over 3,400 elite college students to answer these three questions. It turned out that merely 17% answered all three questions correctly; 23% incorrectly answered one question; 28% incorrectly two; and 33% answered all three wrong. Of all the possible wrong answers, the above intuitive answers—10 cents, 100 minutes, and 24 days—made up the overwhelming majority.

Even for those who made the right answer, the above intuitive answers first appeared in their minds. They had to carefully examine and reflect. For your information, the correct answers are 5 cents, 5 minutes, and 47 days.

Just as ordinary people find it hard to intuitively determine whether 32 X 57 is equal to 1824, these three questions must be calculated by the reflective mind. In math and logic reasoning, intuition is unreliable. The rule of intuition is association, not addition, subtraction, multiplication, and division.

Frederick put these three questions together to form the *Cognitive Reflection Test* that evaluates the degree of reflective thinking and impulsivity. The more correct answers in the test, the more reflective thinking is done and the less impulsive. This also means that the more reflective thinking can correct impulsive instincts.

Frederick found that the results of the *Cognitive Reflection Test* were associated with the performance on several tests that measure general cognitive ability and academic achievement, including the *Wonderlic Personnel Test*, the *Scholastic Achievement Test*, and the *American College Test*. People with higher cognitive ability and achievements are more likely to successfully use reflection to correct the impulsive intuition. Educating the intuitive mind is a fundamental job of the reflective mind.

The "highway" of emotional response

Imagine you are walking in the park or collecting samples of plants and animals in the wild. You suddenly see a tree branch-like, long, slender thing with stripes at your feet. Your immediate reaction is—snake!

Instantly, your breath and heart rate accelerates. Although your brain is blank, you reflexively jump away like an arrow. You run a few more steps, and after assuring yourself it is safe, you look back to the snake. But it stays still and seems motionless. You brace yourself and get a little closer. You look at the thing again with sharper eyes and it turns out to be a dry tree branch. A false alarm.

Joseph E. LeDoux, a neuroscientist at New York University, conducted an in-depth study of this rapid emotional response. He found that the brain structure that plays a central role in this process is the amygdala. The amygdala, an almond-shaped structure, is located deep within the temporal lobe and attached to the end of the hippocampus. It is responsible for the perception of emotional stimuli or cues (particularly negative stimuli related to danger and risk) and making quick and efficient responses.

LeDoux found that in processing emotional information, the amygdala can be activated by two pathways:

- The low-level pathway: Emotional cue → the thalamus (sensory function) → the amygdala → emotional response

- The high-level pathway: Emotional cue → the thalamus → the sensory cortex → the prefrontal cortex (resulting in subjective experience, activation of reflective thinking) → the amygdala → emotional response

The low-level pathway is a "highway." It makes quick and crude judgments and reacts without subjective awareness. The high-level pathway informs our subjective consciousness and makes further adjustments to the reactions of the low-level pathway. The adjustment is slow, but more precise.

The "highway" is fast but at the expense of being error-prone. It requires the more precise albeit slow high-level pathway to double-check it. The image of the branch is roughly analyzed by the thalamus as a snake, which is then transmitted directly to the amygdala. This low-level path causes your quick response—to jump away instantly. After that, the image is sent to the prefrontal cortex for a more accurate analysis. The prefrontal cortex or your consciousness confirms it as a branch and then corrects the previous error signal.

Without the "highway," a tragedy may take place while you wait for the high-level pathway to spend enough time identifying whether it is a snake and dangerous. "Once bitten by a snake, one shies at coiled rope for ten years" or "once bitten, twice shy." The cost of mistaking a rope and a branch as a snake is far smaller than mistaking a snake as a rope or branch.

Nowadays, for many of us, there are few chances of encountering snakes. Rather, we are more likely to encounter strangers. Just like notifying the risk of snakes in the evolutionary history, the amygdala performs the role of alarming a person when encountering strangers.

Psychologists found that when people see a familiar face, the precuneus becomes more active, indicating that people are extracting information from long-term memory and engaging in visual imagination. Here, the activity of the fusiform face area is relatively weak, indicating that it needs less brain activity to recognize a familiar face. But when people see a stranger's face, the fusiform face area and the amygdala become more active, indicating that people are dealing with unfamiliar faces and trying to identify risk and danger. The cautious defense function is automatically activated.

Compared to people with a healthy brain, patients with amygdala damage lose this defense function. They tend to judge unfamiliar faces as trustworthy and are willing to give their property and even life to this person. They also report that if they met the unfamiliar people in the street, they will go and chat.

The two pathways of amygdala correspond to intuition and reflection. Intuition makes quick but rough judgments and emotional reactions to the environment, whereas reflection makes relatively slow but more precise adjustments to emotional responses. Rapid emotional responses are essential to our survival. Our ability to rapidly integrate environmental information and react quickly gives us an advantage in regards to survival and is preserved in evolutionary history. However, this does not mean that rapid emotional reactions will always bring accurate judgments. Sometimes, they cause impulsive reactions.

Impulsive emotions

To make a perfect advertising plan for your new client, you worked hard until midnight one day. You were tired but happy, because you managed to think of a satisfactory one. The next day, however, at the meeting with your client and boss, your partner presented your plan as his own. You feel your blood boiling, and want to question and scold him. You cannot even wait to rush to beat him up. But your boss and the new client are sitting at the other end of the table.

You can obey your emotional reactions and rush to punch him. After all, doing so will signal the sovereignty of your advertising strategy and warn him not to infringe others' interest. But that is likely to result in greater loss: your boss and new client will judge you, not to mention you could do some jail time and get fired.

This is the limitation of automatic, rapid emotional response: the tendency of being impulsive or shortsighted. Emotional responses are generated to protect your values (including motives and goals) involved in a single situation, for instance, the sovereignty of your advertising strategy here. They do not take your long-term values in consideration, such as the trust of your boss and new customers in you and the trust of new clients in your company. Those are the negative repercussions of quick emotional responses.

In the above scenario, the best strategy may be to suppress your anger, sit quietly until the end of the meeting, and talk to your partner. Implementing this strategy requires the participation of your reflective mind. You must use reflection to regulate your anger and suppress your impulses. Otherwise, the situation will only worsen. But as Aristotle said:

"Anybody can become angry—that is easy, but to be angry with the right person and to the right degree and at the right time and for the right purpose, and in the right way—that is not within everybody's power and is not easy."

The following two episodes of emotional outburst in sports history are typical examples where people failed to control their anger.

In the 2006 FIFA World Cup Final, France played against Italy. In the second half of the extra time match, French footballer Zinedine Zidane—then three times FIFA World Player of the Year—had a quarrel with an Italian player. Zidane suddenly head-butted the other's chest and knocked him to the ground. As a result, Zidane was issued a red card.

In the 2007 U.S. baseball game between the Long Island Ducks and Bridgeport Bluefish, Long Island Ducks player Jose Offerman—who had participated in 15 seasons in the Major Leagues and two times all-Star—was hit by a pitch. Offerman exploded. He waved the bat and beat the pitcher and catcher of the other team. The pitcher's one finger was broken and the catcher suffered a severe concussion. Offerman was arrested immediately. He was also suspended indefinitely and has not played professional baseball in the U.S. since then.

Automatic, rapid, emotional reactions are unconscious, intuitive responses, like your anger because of your partner's misconduct and the anger of Zidane and Offerman. Therefore, people must use reflection to analyze and judge the situation and correct and adjust the emotional responses, such as controlling their anger. The secondary adjustment by reflection is of great value to improve the adaptability of emotion. Obviously, Zidane and Offerman failed at this stage.

We become angry because we think someone has done us wrong, whether or not it is true. Anger may be good for protecting these interests. However, often anger worsens the situation and does no good in regards to effective problem-solving. A crude and rapid anger reaction has negative outcomes overall and in the long-term, it requires the slow but precise reflective mind to regulate it. Therefore, when the prefrontal cortex on which reflection depends is impaired, people make dramatically more impulsive reactions in everyday life.

In 1848, in a small town in northeast America, an accidental explosion was caused by a blast during the construction of a railroad. Another 19 years later, safe and convenient explosives would be invented by the Swedish chemist Alfred Nobel (1867). It is conceivable that in 1848 the explosives were not safe and not very convenient for operating.

One day in September that year, when a 25-year-old railway construction worker, Phineas Gage, was using explosives to blast rocks, an unfortunate accidental explosion occurred. An iron bar of 1-meter long and more than 3-centimeters in diameter was jetted out because of the explosion and broke through Gage's head. The iron bar entered from below his left cheekbones, passed through the skull base on the back of the left orbit, and fell on the ground over 20 meters behind him.

Gage was immediately sent to a local hospital. Fortunately, the doctor handled the problem in a timely and appropriate manner. Gage survived and returned to his parents' farm within three months. However, after the accident, Gage was a changed person. His doctor described it:

"The equilibrium or balance, so to speak, between his intellectual faculties and animal propensities, seems to have been destroyed. He is fitful, irreverent, indulging at times in the grossest profanity (which was not previously his custom), manifesting but little deference for his fellows, impatient of restraint or advice when it conflicts with his desires…A child in his intellectual capacity and manifestations, he has the animal passions of a strong man…In this regard his mind was radically changed, so decidedly that his friends and acquaintances said he was 'no longer Gage'."

Because psychology and neuroscience were still in their infancy, scholars could not understand and explain Gage's change. After Gage died, his skull was preserved in the museum. Over 140 years later, Antonio Damasio—the designer of the *Iowa Gambling Task*, whom we met in Chapter 1—and his wife, Hanna Damasio, also a neuroscientist, used 3D reconstruction techniques to study Gage's head. They found that the iron rod that penetrated Gage's head ruined almost the entire left prefrontal cortex. The prefrontal cortex is a major brain region in charge of our reflective mind.

So now, we can easily understand the changes in Gage after the accident. Slow but precise in information processing, the prefrontal cortex is responsible for regulating rapid but crude, impulsive emotional responses initiated by the amygdala. After the prefrontal cortex was damaged, Gage could hardly use his "intellectual faculties" to control "animal propensities" anymore. That was why he became "fitful, irreverent, indulging at times in the grossest profanity…"

Just like Gage, people do not have enough control over their impulsive behaviors when their prefrontal cortex is immature—in the case of children and adolescents—or has limited function—in the case of people with violent tendencies and alcoholics. Psychologists studied teenagers and young adults and found they all have similar emotional reactions to some life events, but their ability to use reflection to regulate their emotional response increases with age. Neuroimaging results suggest this comes with an increased activity associated with the prefrontal cortex.

Irrespective of what kind of facial expressions people see, subjects with frequent violent behaviors have weaker activation of the prefrontal cortex compared to those without violent behaviors. While viewing happy facial expressions in a row, when suddenly being presented a facial expression with neutral emotions, subjects with frequent violent behaviors show persistent activation in the amygdala. An interruption of viewing happy faces may have unconsciously induced anger in these subjects.

In addition, alcohol paralyzes the prefrontal cortex and impairs its normal functioning in inhibiting the activity of the amygdala. Therefore, alcoholism dramatically increases people's impulsive behaviors, leading to fights, domestic violence, murder, and other forms of violence. Reflection predominated by the prefrontal cortex is necessary to effectively regulate the emotional impulses.

Which mind is better?

Reflection is a mode of information processing unique to mankind and represents an evolutionary progress. But *Homo sapiens* only have a history of about 200,000 years. All kinds of advanced animals before humankind have instincts and emotional responses, which is how they have survived until now. These animals appeared at least 200 million (mammals) to 500 million years ago (vertebrates).

Intuition builds on the individual's experience of learning (see Chapter 3). It efficiently guides our daily activities using the rule of association, quick but error-prone. Reflection is based on evidence and logic. It is more accurate than intuition. However, reflection cannot efficiently guide our daily activities because it takes time and effort to collect evidence and do logical reasoning. Both kinds of thinking are essential to human evolution and adaptation.

So, on the question of which mind is better, we can draw two conclusions. First, neither mind is superior to the other, as each has its own strengths and weaknesses. As Seymour Epstein, a psychologist at the University of Massachusetts, put it:

"It is therefore encouraging to realize that since the two systems are independent, improvement in one does not have to be obtained at the expense of improvement in the other. It is therefore to people's advantage to cultivate the desirable attributes of both systems."

Second, the slow and precise reflective mind has the advantage of adjusting the rapid, impulsive, and biased intuition. In our daily lives, perhaps over 80–90% of our decisions are based on intuition, especially in emergent situations and situations we consider relatively insignificant.

On one hand, the impact of these "small" decisions, such as what to eat for each meal, will accumulate. On the other hand, the habit people form while using intuition to decide minor events will inevitably affect their decision-making during major events. Therefore, it is crucial to identify when and where intuition is correct, at what point we can believe them, and when and where it is incorrect and risky. Furthermore, we should also point out what are the specific risks, and how to use reflection to deal with these risks.

Chapter 3. Expert Intuition

The skill of an expert has become a part of him so that he need not know it in consciousness anymore... When things are normal, experts need not solve problems, they need not make any decisions, and their intuition is the feasible solution.

— Hubert L. Dreyfus & Stuart E. Dreyfus, *Mind over Machine. The Power of Human Intuition and Expertise in the Era of the Computer* (1986)

After studying thousands of couples in over three decades, marriage and family psychologist John Gottman at Washington University has been able to predict the "fate" of a couple with great precision. By observing a couple's conversation for merely 5 minutes, Gottman can determine whether they will live in harmony or divorce over a decade later. The accuracy of his prediction is roughly 91%.

Like Gottman, experts in many fields can make such quick and accurate intuitive judgments. In clinical diagnosis, experienced physicians make intuitive assumptions about symptoms within the first few minutes of meeting with a patient, guessing one or several diseases. They use these assumptions to guide the subsequent inquiries and examinations, and use the new information to test their hypotheses or make differential diagnoses. The intuitive assumptions of experienced doctors are often highly accurate.

These experts' quick and intuitive judgments are essentially the same as the intuition of ordinary people. Both are unconscious and we do not know their early stages of information processing (raw materials and operations). However, in most cases, in the specialized areas, expert intuition is far more accurate than ordinary people's intuition. Therefore, understanding the rationale behind expert intuition and how experts use it can help us improve the accuracy of our daily intuition.

Chess masters

Imagine the case of blindfolded chess player. Players usually sit with their back facing the board and someone else moves the pieces for them. They must remember the position of all the pieces on the board in their minds. Chess masters can play many boards of blindfolded chess simultaneously. In 1937, George Koltanowski, an American chess grandmaster, created a world record for blindfolded chess. He could play 34 games at the same time, winning 24 and drawing 10 in 13.5 hours. Koltanowski must have super working memory, otherwise, how can he achieve such a result?

Chess masters like him, after looking at a board, should be able to remember the location of many pieces. To see if this is the case, Herbert Simon—the computer scientist and psychologist who made a landmark report at the 1956 MIT conference that marked the cognitive revolution—conducted a classic study with chess players.

Simon asked a master, a Class A player (whose chance of beating a master is estimated to be around one in one thousand), and a beginner to spend 5 seconds looking at a board and then reproduce it. In five different chess sets which had about 24–26 pieces each, the master could on average reconstruct 16 pieces correctly; the Class A player 8 pieces; the beginner 4 pieces. However, when viewing a board that was randomized and totally out of the logic of chess, the number of pieces that could be correctly placed by all of them was no more than 4 pieces.

Therefore, it is not that the memory of the masters is enormous, but that their ability to use the limited conscious working memory to deal with meaningful pieces or so-called "chunks" is excellent. Using eye-tracking technology, psychologists have found that masters look at the board in a chunk manner by associating pieces of confrontation, proximity, or the like with each other. They process and store the information of the pieces in chunks and when asked to reproduce a board, they put the pieces on the board in this chunk way.

Recall the magic number seven. Masters' conscious working memory does not differ from ordinary people; they also can only process seven items at a time. But through chunking, they can unite a massive amount of information into one chunk and then process seven chunks at a time. This greatly expands their information processing capacity. Research shows that one chunk used by chess masters usually contains 2–4 pieces and sometimes 6–8 or even up to 15 pieces.

Reflection is largely constrained by the limited conscious working memory. However, with their chunking strategies, after extensive training, experts can freely access the chunked information from long-term memory and transfer it quickly to working memory. So, to the average person, experts seem to have unlimited working memory. Simon's student K. Anders Ericsson, a psychologist at Florida State University, calls this working memory "long-term working memory."

Psychologists have found that whereas Class A players usually store about 1,000 chunks in their long-term memory, masters store up to 10,000–100,000 chunks. No wonder a grandmaster can relocate 16 pieces correctly after merely viewing the board for 5 seconds.

Now let's consider another question: how do the masters think when playing chess? Do they move every piece by using the 7 steps of reflection? Do they first figure out as many strategies as possible, and then compare and choose the best?

Psychologists used a "think aloud" method to let the chess masters report every thought that occurs in their mind during chess games. Surprisingly, the masters seldom adopted reflective strategies. Of 40 games, in only 5 the masters used reflective strategies, at which time they would come up with multiple strategies and choose the best one. At other times, the masters all used the first strategy that occurred to them. In other words, they play instinctively. They usually think of the first strategy intuitively and then use "mental simulation" to evaluate it.

Mental simulation means they assume making that move and consider the later series of actions and the potential outcomes. It is a hypothetical thinking that depends on the reflective mind. If the expected outcome is satisfactory, they make that move; if not, they evaluate other intuitive moves. Thus, the strategies used by the masters are actually a combination of intuition and reflection. They first intuitively think of a solution and then use reflection to judge it.

A study using magnetoencephalography (MEG) found that, when viewing a chess board, the prefrontal and parietal cortex of top-ranked players were more active, indicating that they were extracting information from the long-term memory and processing it. In contrast, the medial temporal cortex of lower ranked players was more active, indicating that they were coding new information. This differentiated pattern of brain activation is consistent with the observation that top-ranked players identify chunks from their long-term memory more often. This chunk (or pattern) recognition is the source of intuition for chess masters.

The chunk recognition strategy from long-term memory is fast, efficient, and effortless. Psychologists found that limiting the time duration of a move from 2 minutes to 6 seconds does not affect the quality of each move in the masters, but severely impairs the quality of each move in Class B players. Looking at a new game, the masters can focus on the most crucial pieces within 2 seconds. This explains why even after considering other moves, masters often use the first intuitive move: their first intuitive move is often the most optimal one.

Fire chief

When decision-making psychologist Gary Klein interviewed another fire chief who had over 20 years of professional experience, the interview apparently did not go well.

Klein asked the chief to describe a challenging firefighting event; the chief said he did not remember any. Klein let him recall some difficult decisions and the chief only looked blankly at him. Klein asked the chief to think of some fire incidents that show the importance of firefighting experience; the chief simply appeared puzzled.

Klein gave up asking and let the chief describe the decision-making process in a recent firefighting experience. The chief mentioned a fire one week ago, but he claimed that he "did not make any decisions" during that fire. Klein asked him to describe the fire process.

The chief said it was a simple family fire that took place in a freestanding home. He rushed to the scene and saw the fire and smoke emerging from the back of the house. He immediately thought the origin of the fire was in the kitchen. He walked around to check the fire and then told the firefighters to prepare to enter the house from the front door with a 1.75-inch hose.

When he walked around the house after a lap and confirmed everything, he immediately ordered the firefighters to act. The firefighters connected the hoses to a nearby fire hydrant and rushed into the room. They sprayed water towards the kitchen and quickly extinguished the fire.

Then, the chief looked towards Klein and said, "See, I did not make any decisions."

This time, it was Klein's turn to look befuddled. He asked the chief, usually when a house is on fire, everyone runs out of it, why did you let firefighters go inside the house? Why not spray water directly from the back of the house? The chief glanced at Klein and said spraying water from the outside would only make the fire spread inside the house. It would be better to go in and drive the fire out. However, the fire chief added that if there were other buildings or flammable structures outside the house, it would have been a different story.

The chief did make the choice and decision, although he himself did not realize it. The chief came to the solution so natural, quick and effortless. He did not use the 7 steps of reflective thinking to find many solutions and choose the best one. He used intuition, or more specifically, expert intuition, like the instincts used by chess masters.

Klein's extensive study of fire chiefs found they rarely use what we call reflection. They usually think briefly, for a few seconds or less. They think about one solution only at a time and assess whether it works. If the expected outcome of the solution is satisfactory, they will use it. If not, they improve it. If it is difficult to improve, they move on to the next most likely solution.

Like the chess masters, the fire chiefs usually figure out the first solution intuitively and then use mental simulation to evaluate the solution. They imagine themselves implementing the solution to see if there will be problems. This way, they eventually, but quickly, come up with a workable solution.

However, what makes them professional is that the first solution they consider is often an optimal one. It is the best match they have identified from their experience stored in the long-term memory, inspired by environmental cues. Klein called this decision-making method "recognition-primed decision-making" (hereinafter referred to as recognition decision).

Like the chunks used by chess masters, abundant patterns are stored in the fire chiefs' long-term memory. They can usually predict how a fire spreads in a building, what signs predict the collapse of a house, how much water can extinguish a fire of a particular size, when it is necessary to call for assistance, and when to urgently evacuate.

For example, the fire chief above saw the smoke coming out of the back of the house and knew that the fire was in the kitchen and immediately thought of entering the house from the front door and extinguishing the fire with a 1.75-inch hose. That intuition resulted from over 20 years of professional experience. He knew what happened, and the different effects of spraying water in and out of the house.

The intuition of the fire chief who saved his own and colleagues' lives in Chapter 1 was also one such recognition decision. Quiet kitchen, hot living room, no expected outcome with spraying water towards the kitchen. The chief's intuition, inspired by these environmental clues, was "feel strange" and "get out of here NOW!"

Klein's survey showed that in 81.4% of cases, the fire chiefs were using this recognition decision. In only 11.5% of the cases, they compared several alternatives. In the other 7.1% of the cases, they tried to come up with a new solution.

Expert intuition "is nothing but recognition"

Klein and other researchers conducted similar studies on managers, pilots, pediatric nurses, engineers, and war commanders and all confirmed the above findings. In most cases, the experts rely on recognition decision. In military decisions, the proportion of recognition decision can be as high as 96%. The following features characterize the situations in which experts highly rely on recognition decision:

- Under time pressure

- At high stakes

- In highly experienced field

- In dynamic situations where things change rapidly and substantially

- With inadequate information such as loss of communication or information being vague

- Without clear goals, namely being unable to establish evaluation criteria

Only when the experts need to justify or confirm their choices, resolve conflicts, optimize, and decide in complex situations, will they use reflective strategies to compare multiple solutions.

Unlike experts, novices rely on reflective strategies in over 50% of their decisions. It is partly because novices do not have enough knowledge or patterns stored in their long-term memory for recognition. And that is why novices often make decisions slower and less accurately than experts.

The operation principle of intuition is association. In decision-making and problem-solving, the best association is based on recognition—pattern recognition—from one's experience and knowledge. This is where the essence of expert intuition lies. As Herbert Simon put it:

"Long experience leads to chunking, so that familiar patterns emerging in a situation immediately suggest a possible move (chess), a possible condition (medical diagnosis), a possible fault (electronic troubleshooting)... Such associations evolve over time and persist because they contribute to success in problem solving. The chunking process reinforces this persistance. Therefore...intuition is not a magical sixth sense; it is a sophisticated form of reasoning based on chunking that an expert hones over years of job-specific experience.

"When an expert resolves or answers a question extremely fast, and he himself cannot describe the process of thinking, we call the expert's reaction 'intuition.' The situation has provided a cue; this cue

has given the expert access to information stored in memory, and the information provided the answer. Intuition is nothing more and nothing less than recognition."

If we look at this process from the paradigm of information processing, three steps are involved in generating an expert intuition:

- Environmental cues enter sensory memory;

- The cues automatically identify the solution from long-term memory;

- The identified solution appears in working memory and consciousness in the form of gut feelings.

The precise prediction of the marriage and family psychologist John Gottman also comes from his recognition decision. When observing a couple's communication, he automatically identifies the following patterns:

- Opening fire (conversations start with criticism or sarcasm);

- Four wicked knights: criticism (on one's personality), contempt (insult and cynicism, such as hostile humor), defensiveness (self-protection), and stonewalling (refusal to communicate);

- Flooding (hyper-vigilance);

- Physiological markers including red face, accelerated heart rate, fight or flight;

- The lack of the attempt to repair contradictions, or the attempts to repair contradictions failed;

- Full of bad memories;

- Indifference and alienation.

A psychologist has been quoted to have said this of his ex-wife:

"I used to live with a woman who blamed me for everything. The hotel was unpalatable, the plane was late, and even the folds on her dry-cleaning pants she blames on me. One day I said, 'My dear, you are the person who I've ever seen most likely to have external attribution on the bad.' 'Yes,' she shouted, 'that's all your fault!'"

This kind of attributing everything to the external and blaming her husband is a manifestation of self-protection (defense) and strongly implies criticism.

Shouting to open a dialogue satisfied the feature of opening fire, hysterical explosion, and physiological markers. Obviously, from this short confession, she did not try to reconcile contradictions. It seems that Gottman's module does have predictive power, as this couple finally got divorced.

Physicians also use recognition decisions. During their long-term learning and training, a series of recognition modules are formed by the types of diseases, pathology, clinical manifestations, developmental courses, and differential diagnoses. Novices typically have less experience and their knowledge is limited. Most symptoms and illnesses they have learned are limited to the classic cases introduced in textbooks. These cases are isolated from one another and lack connection.

Experts are more experienced and consequently have more extensive and accurate knowledge. They can identify various typical, atypical, and fuzzy cases and form more diagnostic chunks. Experts are well aware of the differences and linkages between various cases and on top of this rich knowledge base, they can easily make diagnoses and differential diagnoses by recognition.

Congenital heart disease, for example, can be divided into two categories according to skin color: non-cyanotic and cyanotic. The former include atrial septal defect (ASD), endocardial cushion defect (ECD), and partial anomalous pulmonary venous connection (PAPVC). The latter includes total anomalous pulmonary venous connection (TAPVC) and others. This is a classic textbook categorization and novices can generally grasp these differences.

Experts, however, will also notice that the four diseases, ASD, ECD, PAPVC, and TAPVC all simultaneously manifest as an increase in blood flow to the right of the heart. So the experts consider them together as a new module for diagnosis and treatment. This is just one example of how experts form various chunks.

When can we trust expert intuition?

Not all expert intuition is equal.

Consider the Long-Term Capital Management (LTCM) of the 1990s. LTCM was a hedge fund with an all-star team including two famous economists (Myron Scholes and Robert Merton), a former vice-chairman of the Federal Reserve (David Mullins), and several highly experienced traders. It had averaged over 40% annual return (after tax) in the first few years and quickly became the darling of the financial world.

Unfortunately, in less than four months after the Russian economic crisis in 1998, the company lost 4.6 billion U.S. dollars and soon collapsed. Ironically, in the previous year, the two famous economists, Scholes and Merton, had just been awarded the Nobel Prize in economics for their work on controlling financial risk. Here, the top teams of LTCM used not only their instincts but also sophisticated, Nobel Prize level mathematical calculations. But these did not prevent it from "sinking."

Next, consider the 2008 financial crisis that swept the globe, beginning in the United States. Many economists attribute responsibility to Alan Greenspan, former Chairman of the Federal Reserve from 1987 to 2006. His long-term policy of low interest rate exacerbated the housing bubble and he failed to control the issuance of high-risk, deceptive mortgage loans. Greenspan, who was widely considered the "Economic Sage" and "the greatest banker of all time," confessed to the U.S. Congress that:

"This crisis has turned out to be much broader than anything I could have imagined...I made a mistake in presuming that the self-interest of organizations, specifically banks, is such that they were best capable of protecting shareholders and equity in the firms..."

Gary Klein and another decision-making psychologist at Princeton University, Nobel laureate of economics in 2002, Daniel Kahneman concluded that the first prerequisite for accurate expert intuition is:

The environment can provide cues that effectively represent the current situation

"Effectively" means "there is a steady relationship between the cues and the next events, or between the cues and the result of the solutions." These cues are the basis which experts rely on to identify chunks. This requires the environment to be relatively stable, regular, and predictable. Like the examples of LTCM and Greenspan, it is difficult to get accurate expert intuition in stock investment and forecasting of major economic and political events because of their complex and changing circumstances.

However, in the areas of firefighting, health care and medicine, weather forecasting, aeronautical flying, and driving, people often find reliable expert intuition because of the relative stability and predictability of the situation. Some tend to think weather forecasts are inaccurate. But studies have found that forecasters' accuracy in predicting the short-term weather, such as temperatures and precipitation within 24 hours, is usually very high.

Now it is understandable why, compared to novices, experts spend more time checking the situation and evaluating the environment. Environmental cues are a prerequisite for accurate intuition.

In addition, Klein and Kahneman found that accurate expert intuition still requires a second condition:

People must have proper opportunities to learn these cues

In response to these cues, people should have sufficient reserve of chunks and patterns in their long-term memory. In the process of learning the value of environmental cues, the key is to obtain accurate and timely feedback about one's intuition. Continued access to this kind of high-quality feedback is a prerequisite for the accurate stock of knowledge in long-term memory.

In the early detection of breast cancer, radiologists usually make a diagnosis based on mammograms. A study by Craig Beam, a statistician at the University of South Florida, however, found no correlation between the total number of radiographs read by radiologists and the accuracy of their diagnosis. In fact, the accuracy of their diagnostic readings after residency training had been declining at an average rate of 0.76% per year.

What is going on here? Why did more experienced radiologists have a lower accuracy of diagnosis?

Simply put, their experiences are not necessarily valuable ones. Radiologists rarely receive timely and valid feedback after reading an X-ray and making a diagnosis. Follow-up diagnosis of breast cancer is mainly the work of the breast and thyroid specialists. These follow-up diagnostic results are usually not communicated to radiologists. This means that radiologists do not even know they have made a wrong diagnosis. Without feedback, they eventually lose the basis for judging right and wrong, and fail to learn from their successes and failures.

Interestingly, in the above study, the accuracy of radiologists in hospitals practicing dual-readership was higher than those in hospitals without such policies. Dual-readership is a two-way feedback method that provides a learning opportunity for the radiologists.

In contrast, surgeons, such as oncologists, often get rapid feedback during and after surgeries. They can learn from their decisions. For surgeons, the total number of operations is positively associated with their quality of surgery and postoperative care.

Practice makes perfect, but only when you practice like an expert

We now know that the quick, precise intuition of experts originates in their method of pattern recognition, which essentially depends on two aspects.

First, they have sufficient knowledge in their long-term memory, so they can see patterns and trends in things that novices cannot see. The experts have an overall grasp of the situation, and know various possible strategies and their corresponding effects. These are the core sources of information for pattern recognition and mental simulation.

Second, they can obtain accurate, comprehensive, and representative cues from the environment, and then use these cues to identify solutions from long-term memory. The result of such identification appears as intuition.

Expert intuition and the intuition of ordinary people are essentially the same. Both are an information processing mode, the early stages of which we subjectively do not know. But ordinary intuition is less accurate as it is more likely to be based on biased, incomplete, and unrepresentative cues in the environment and insufficient knowledge in the long-term memory. This tells us a shortcut towards more accurate intuition: achieving expert intuition in a certain area.

To achieve expert intuition, we must learn like an expert, namely learn about cue-outcome associations by getting timely and valid feedback. Meanwhile, we must practice and accumulate. Marriage and family psychologist John Gottman spent over 30 years researching couples. Fire chiefs and expert physicians often have decades of professional experience.

As mentioned earlier, Class A chess players have about 1,000 chunks stored in their long-term memory, while masters have as many as 10,000–100,000 chunks.

The former requires about 1,000 to 5,000 hours of specialized training, and the latter 10,000 (5 hours a day for 6 years) to 50,000 hours (5 hours a day for 30 years).

However, unlike the domain-general reflection (logic applies universally), expert intuition is domain-specific. It is limited to the area of expertise in which training and learning are conducted. Having expert performance and expert intuition in one area does not guarantee the same levels of performance and intuition in other areas. When decision problems deviate from an expert's own area, their performance and intuition are usually no more accurate than an average person's is.

Whereas it is impossible to have expert intuition in all areas of decision-making, perhaps we can learn like an expert in all areas: setting clear goals and criteria for each decision and obtaining accurate, timely, and diagnostic feedback. We can learn like experts, and constantly expand our library of knowledge and experience. In this way, we can move towards more accurate intuition.

Chapter 4. Personal Preference: The Expert Intuition of Ordinary People

The heart has its reasons which reason does not know.

— Blaise Pascal, *Pensées [Thoughts]* (1670)

A real estate broker noticed an interesting phenomenon. When buying a house, people emphasize everything they want at the beginning, vividly portraying the type of house they like. But often, in the end, they choose a house different from what they originally described. So the broker simply patiently listens to people and sympathetically looks into their eyes. Then, she takes them to see a variety of houses, including those they dislike in theory.

A couple said they wanted to buy an old house in the city, because they liked the classic style. But when the broker took them to see a nice, new house, they became excited. They ended up buying a new home in the suburbs. This phenomenon is even nicknamed "the buyer's lie" by real estate brokers.

So, are people really lying?

Organizers of speed dating have also found a similar phenomenon. Before a speed dating event, people are asked to describe the type they like and to use the 1 (worst) to 10 (best) ruler to rate their requirements on attractiveness, common interests, humor, sincerity, intelligence, ambition, etc. But, like people who buy a house, participants in speed dating are often inconsistent: what they say they like does not agree with what they like after meeting potential partners.

A woman "vowed" to say she liked smart and honest men. But when she met an attractive, humorous but not so smart and honest man at a speed dating event, she found herself fascinated by and almost crazy about him. That moment she changed her idea of what kind of man she liked. The question still remains, what kind of man does she like?

Are the types of houses people describe when looking to buy a property wrong? Is devising a list of attributes of desired romantic partners before a speed dating event wrong? Perhaps not wrong, but incomplete is the better word. Although people's description of their preference may already be the best understanding of their reflective mind, often, it is unreliable. Because preference and love are determined by the unconscious and intuition. The conscious and reflective mind know only part of it.

Does love need a reason?

People in love should all have this experience. At the beginning of a romantic relationship, one is likely to ask the other, "Why do you love me? What part of me do you love the best?" At this moment, the one being asked often, to give the answer (perhaps also to give oneself an answer), thinks hard. Ultimately (the sooner the better), one should give a "fair and reasonable" answer. The motives behind such Q & A activities are easy to understand. But the question is, to what extent is the "fair and reasonable" answer accurate? In reality, the answer to this question may not be satisfactory. Because people may not consciously know exactly why they love someone: affection is intuitive.

Generally, the quality of a couple's romantic relationship, or how happy and satisfied they feel towards each other, is a reliable predictor of the sustainability of their relationship. A study by Timothy D. Wilson, a psychologist at the University of Virginia, found that in a group of couples dating more than half a year, the association between their reported quality of the relationship and whether they would break up 8–9 months later was 0.56. The higher quality the relationship, the less likely couples break up. Fair enough.

However, a later finding went beyond Wilson's expectation. He recruited another group of couples and before asking them to report their quality of the relationship, he let them analyze their relationship and explain why they loved each other. Surprisingly, when Wilson tried to relate the quality of relationship with whether they broke up 8–9 months later, he detected no statistically significant association. The quality of love reported by the couples did not matter if they broke up 8–9 months later. Strange.

Why, after reflectively analyzing and explaining the relationship, does the quality of love that people subjectively reported become irrelevant if they break up?

From the perspective of reflection, people generally evaluate the quality of love based on their own analysis of the relationship. Therefore, the reason is likely to be the reflective thinking they engaged in.

Wilson looked further at the contents of the couples' analysis. The degree of affection shown in people's analysis was positively associated with their reported quality of love, which is entirely understandable. The more reasons for love, the more love and the higher the quality of love. However, affection demonstrated in the analysis was also irrelevant in regards to whether they would break up after 8–9 months.

If you are asked to analyze your romantic relationship, how will you do it? Think about it, why do you want to be with your partner? Why do you love him/her?

Perhaps you may think this is 30% because the other is sincere, 20% smart, 20% humorous, 20% you have similar character and interest, and the remaining 10% because of the appearance of the other...

Like people's description of their preference when buying a house and speed dating, the reasons people think of when analyzing their relationship are not wrong and baseless. However, they may not be the exact reason they fell in love with each other originally. The latter is often unconscious and intuitive. People often "feel" attracted by the other one and fall in love with him/her.

This is actually the contradiction between reflection and intuition. First, reflective analysis needs to rely on language. So the reasons given by reflective analysis are also discursive. But people cannot reasonably speak all their feelings or know all the factors that determine how they feel. The reasons people "weave" for their own feelings are often just their own perception of those feelings and the parts easily verbalized. We often have complicated feelings we cannot describe to others well, don't we?

Second, reflective analysis requires the use of raw material information. But this information must be easily recalled. In a certain situation, we can only make reflection using information easily remembered, or easily extracted from long-term memory. However, the information we recall easily is not comprehensive and representative because our memories are easily influenced by other unrelated factors.

Why did we think of sincerity, intelligence, and humor when analyzing the reasons for our love? That was, at least partially, because someone else had mentioned them earlier (e.g., the organizer of the speed dating event) and they naturally spring into the mind and attract our attention. Information we have been exposed to earlier affects our subsequent memory or to what extent we can recall certain information.

Third, during reflection, people will be unconsciously influenced by social expectations. We often check ourselves from the perspective of others, which makes us unconsciously follow others' preference.

Wilson examined the reasons the above couples wrote and found they fit all three characteristics. They are easily verbalized, easily remembered, and appear to be reasonable and in line with social expectations. As a result, people's reflection of their love is no longer accurate and cannot reflect their true feelings. Often, this kind of reflection misleads people's choices and decisions because people obey the result of their reflection and change their attitude after analysis.

In another study, Wilson asked people to rate five paintings. Two were Monet and van Gogh's artworks and the other three were humorous cartoons or animal pictures. People had to intuitively judge how much they liked or disliked each painting, and then choose one to take home. Most people commented that they preferred art painting and eventually 95% brought the art painting back home, while only 5% took the humorous painting home. Wilson's follow-up survey found that people were still satisfied with their choice 3–4 weeks later.

However, similar to the previous study of the couples, Wilson asked another group of subjects to think about why they liked or disliked each painting and write down the reasons. As a result, far more subjects commented that they preferred humorous painting and as much as 36%—well above the 5% in people who did not analyze the reasons—chose a humorous painting to take home. A follow-up survey found that after 3–4 weeks, those who chose humorous paintings were more likely to be dissatisfied with the painting they chose. This happened primarily in subjects with little artistic knowledge.

People could make satisfactory choices when judging their preferences based on pure feelings. Most people preferred art paintings without analyzing the reason why, and 95% took the art painting home. However, after analyzing the reasons for their preference, many changed their initial attitude, especially those who lacked artistic knowledge. They mistakenly thought they liked humorous painting and 36% brought the humorous painting back home.

Again, the reason for this phenomenon is related to the reasons people analyze. Why people like a particular piece of art is not easily verbalized, especially for those who lack knowledge of arts. Relatively speaking, humorous pictures are different, as people are very apt to give specific reasons for liking them.

When seeing a painting depicting a cat standing on a fence and saying "step by step," people will be happy and clearly aware of why they are happy. On the contrary, although people like a piece of art such as Monet's *Water Lilies* or van Gogh's *Irises*, they generally cannot say why, because people's love of artistic works is usually intuitive and based on the overall sensual beauty.

Wilson's analysis of the reasons reported by people found they gave more reasons for humor than art. For those who analyzed reasons and lacked artistic knowledge, their reflective evaluation was more likely to be inconsistent with their initial intuitive preference. They were more likely to change their attitude and obey their reflective evaluation.

However, when people took the painting home, they rarely analyzed the reasons for their love. Soon, the reasons they analyzed were forgotten. Their initial intuitive preference would come back to haunt them, leaving them regretful of their choice. People with artistic knowledge, on the other hand, differed in that they clearly understood their criteria of evaluation and selection and were not easily affected by the analysis.

It seems that the reason we like something is often unclear to our reflective thinking and consciousness. In short, we can say that love may not need a reason, at least it need not be analyzed by the reflective mind.

Ordinary people's "expert intuition"

This personal preference choice is a subconscious choice and needs to rely on intuition. We make this kind of choice every day, and soon we know whether our choices are what we like or not. We can get timely and accurate feedback on our choices. Thus, we have enough knowledge—although unconscious—of our preferences. Personal preference is actually an "expert intuition" in our daily life.

We have satisfied one prerequisite for accurate expert intuition: sufficient storage of knowledge in our long-term memory. So to get accurate expert intuition, we just need to obtain accurate, comprehensive, and representative cues of the available options. The cues then automatically activate our preferred patterns and the latter occurs to us as intuition. This intuition is an accurate expert intuition that balances all previous knowledge reserves and leads to a satisfactory outcome.

In the *Iowa Gambling Task* we introduced in Chapter 1, people's intuitive feeling of risk before reaching the disadvantageous decks is an expert intuition. That intuition is guided by the feedback of winning and losing following each card: winning and losing fall in the category of personal preference. Notably, patients with lesions of the ventromedial prefrontal cortex (vmPFC) fail to show that intuition in the *Iowa Gambling Task*. They continue to draw cards from the two disadvantageous decks despite there are plenty of opportunities for them to learn. The vmPFC is a brain region known to weigh objects on a common currency of value. That is, the vmPFC encodes personal preference. Without the direction of personal preference, people's normal choices that rely on intuitive feelings lose their insight.

Similarly, the formation of first impressions of people we encountered in Chapter 2 falls under this kind of intuition. Neuroscientists have found that the amygdala is active in the formation of first impressions. The amygdala is the brain structure that governs the highway of emotional responses. This indicates that in the formation of first impressions, people use emotional judgments. So the formation of first impressions is actually a judgment based on personal preference.

After watching the teachers' three 2-second silent videos, the students could make a reasonably accurate evaluation of their teaching effectiveness including personality. First, the information in these video clips reflects the teacher's abilities and characteristics. Non-verbal behaviors reflect people's true features, inner thoughts, and personalities. This satisfies one condition of accurate expert intuition: the environment provides effective cues reflecting the situation.

Second, people know what to read from these video clips. We have enough experience interacting with others because in real life, we deal with strangers almost daily. We unconsciously make judgments about strangers and then obtain timely feedback about those judgments. We constantly correct previous intuition and are given continued opportunities to learn from our experiences. This satisfies the second condition of accurate expert intuition.

Psychologists find that people automatically categorize new, unfamiliar things into one of their familiar categories without subjective awareness and make quick judgments of good or bad, like or dislike. The moment we see a person, we not only see this person is a man, but also see him as handsome; not only see this person is a woman, but also see her as beautiful. The moment we see them, we see them as kind, intelligent, and sincere (or the inverse).

So, like experts of chess masters and fire chiefs, we are actually using automatic recognition and classification. We make recognition decisions in terms of preferences. These are our "expert intuition."

When reflection hurts

After he graduated from Cambridge in 1831, Charles Darwin received a letter from his botanist teacher John Henslow. It said that the captain of HMS *Beagle*, Robert FitzRoy, was recruiting a young volunteer as a naturalist to explore South America. Henslow thought that was a good opportunity and recommended Darwin apply. Darwin went to see Captain FitzRoy for an interview. Interestingly, Darwin was almost rejected because of the shape of his nose.

It turned out that Captain FitzRoy believed he could judge people's character by observing their appearance, particularly their nose.

"He doubted whether anyone with my nose could possess sufficient energy and determination for the voyage," Darwin wrote in his autobiography.

Since psychological research on the formation of first impressions would take over another century to develop, Captain FitzRoy obviously had no way of knowing the importance of gathering sufficient information. He did not know that intuition after a comprehensive collection of information was accurate. But fortunately, after gathering more information, the captain dismissed this original suspicion and accepted Darwin as the naturalist of the *Beagle*.

When we see a person, we seem to intuitively see their mind. In using this kind of expert intuition, we not only rely on the shape of a person's nose, their height, hairstyle, and eyes to judge his personality, but also rely on their overall body language and how they act, including facial expressions, conversations, and behaviors, among other things.

People do not know exactly how to make impressions and judgments of others in their subjective consciousness. Therefore, just like the negative outcomes of analyzing why does one love their romantic partner and prefer a certain object over another, analyzing one's impression of a stranger makes people come to inaccurate conclusions. This is exactly the characteristic of ordinary people's expert intuition— personal preference: reflection impairs the accuracy of intuition.

Harvard psychologist Ambady took the same three 10-second videos to another group of college students to watch. Before they evaluated the effectiveness of the teachers, Ambady asked them to spend 1 minute analyzing why they thought the teachers were effective in teaching and write all the reasons down. The final accuracy of the judgment of this group of students became substantially lower: the correlation coefficient between their judgment and the evaluation of the students that had listened to the teacher for a whole semester was only 0.27, much smaller than the previous 0.71.

In these personal preferences and choices, there are at least three reasons why reflection hurts. First, to make decisions using reflection, the reflective mind should be guided by personal preferences and values (including motives and goals). Yet, often, our conscious mind is not aware of our internal preferences and values. The latter is mostly learned by trial-and-error throughout our life experiences and thus remains unconscious.

The reflective mind cannot know all the elements that determine intuition, so our "rational mind" will bring the feeling into a "sampling trap:" it can only access part of the factors that determine intuition among a pool. Unrepresentative local information causes bias. Many factors affect whether a certain piece of information will be sampled by the reflective mind. In Wilson's experiment above, information easily verbalized, recalled, and met the expectations of others, were more likely to enter the couples' mind for reflection on their love.

A well-known social psychologist was considering whether or not to move to another university. But that was not an easy decision because both her current university and the university she was thinking of had advantages and disadvantages. She tried to use Franklin's list of pros and cons (Chapter 1) to more clearly compare the two, but halfway through her analysis, she found herself shouting, "Oh, that's not right. I have to add a few more good reasons to the other column."

What is the problem here?

Her intuition told her she preferred one university, but she listed more advantages for another university. If she trusted her reflective mind, she would have entered the sampling trap.

The second reason that reflection hurts is the conscious working memory we use for reflection is limited. Sometimes, because we cannot effectively consider multiple factors at the same time, our reflection leads us to emphasize a few features. In this way, we lose our insight of the big picture and get farther away from optimal decisions.

The third reason is that like Darwin's captain, people's reflection often contains false logic. Using the wrong logic for reflection cannot get accurate conclusions.

Then in what kind of situation can reflection contribute? The answer is for problems related to facts and numbers.

Research shows that on tasks such as answering how long a river is, how much tobacco is consumed annually, the circulation of a magazine and the size of a country, analyzing reasons helps to improve people's performance so that their estimation gets closer to the truth. Besides, for mathematical problems such as the *Cognitive Reflection Test* we introduced in Chapter 2, reflection is the key towards getting correct answers.

Give intuition some time: the science of unconscious thought

So far, we have not distinguished between different types of intuition. General intuition can be thought of as an instantaneous instinct after encountering a problem. There is little time between the need to decide and what we may call "immediate intuition."

Yet another kind of intuition is "sleeping on it" as it's commonly called. For a given problem, we let the unconscious handle it and instead turn our attention to other things; some time later, we decide. Ap Dijksterhuis, a psychologist at the University of Amsterdam in the Netherlands, calls it "unconscious thought." Unlike immediate intuition, unconscious thought gives the brain a certain amount of time to subconsciously manipulate information, or "incubate," and later get the result from intuition. During this time, the brain shifts its subjective consciousness elsewhere, to other activities as usual.

Dijksterhuis found that in complex situations where people have to make choices based on a large amount of information, unconscious thought often brings better decisions than reflective thinking.

Suppose you just arrived in a new city. You need to rent a house. There are three apartment rooms for you to choose:

- The first room is in a good location and close to the supermarket. The landlord and the neighbors are kind, but it is kind of noisy, as sometimes you hear the cars on the streets outside. The room is not large. The window faces north so there is no sunshine coming in.

- The second room is close to the supermarket, but the landlord is not very friendly. The neighbors are not bad. It is quiet and the room is large, so you have enough space. The window faces west and in the afternoon, there is sunshine.

- The third room is also close to the supermarket. The window faces east, so you can enjoy the sunshine in the morning. It is somewhat noisy. The landlord and neighbors are not very friendly and the room is not large.

How would you choose? If you use Franklin's list of pros and cons, think about how you give each factor weight. Are you willing to endure noise and no sunshine for the convenience of shopping? Would you endure noise and unfriendly landlords and neighbors just to see the sunshine in the morning?

Dijksterhuis designed four apartment rooms A, B, C and D. Each apartment has 12 descriptions. Room A and C had 6 positive and 6 negative features; B had 8 positive and 4 negative features; D had 4 positive and 8 negative features. A pilot survey showed that experts and ordinary people generally think room B is the best, D is the worst, and A and C are in the middle.

Dijksterhuis used a computer screen to present the description of each room in a random order and let them evaluate each using a scale of 1–10. 1 means very bad and 10 very good. After that, they had to choose their favorite.

For the first group of subjects, before making the judgment, they needed to think for 3 minutes. This was the Reflective Thinking (RT) group. It was 3 minutes because most of the subjects thought this amount of time was sufficient to make such judgments.

The second group was the Unconscious Thought (UT) group. They were asked to do a working memory task for 3 minutes, after which they had to make the judgments. The complex task took the subjects' full attention so they had no energy to engage in any conscious thinking during that period.

Dijksterhuis found that whereas 47% of subjects in the RT group chose the best room, 60% of those in the UT group did so. And while both groups rated room B as the best, D the worst, and A and C in the middle, the UT group was better at distinguishing the best from the worst room: they rated the best room far better than the worst one.

In addition, most subjects in the RT group reported that their choice was based on one or two selection criteria. Those in the UT group were more likely to report they tried to judge as a whole and use all the information. The latter kind of information processing helped to polarize the options and made it easier to choose.

People who have ever rented or bought a house have a similar experience. This decision-making process is very brain savvy. It consumes much effort and is far more complex than the mathematical operations we mentioned in Chapter 2. However, laborious reflection often results in less satisfactory results. In contrast, unconscious thought is effortless and allows the brain to carry out other activities; yet, it brings better decision-making outcomes than reflection. Extraordinary.

Dijksterhuis and other researchers found similar phenomena in the decision-making process of selecting cars, notebooks, backpacks, holiday packages, and roommates. The UT group consistently made superior choice than the RT group.

To find out why the UT group made better judgments, in a study of choosing roommates, researchers asked subjects to quickly indicate each piece of information that belonged to which roommate. Interestingly, the results showed that compared to the RT group, the UT group could identify the positive features of the best roommate and the negative features of the worst roommate more accurately and faster.

The UT group subconsciously polarized the information so they could clearly distinguish the positive from the negative options and form a more integrated overall impression of each option.

Since there is a prolonged period of time to process information in a polarized manner, information can be better integrated and compared to make more informed judgments and choices.

Interestingly, unconscious thought requires a goal-oriented approach. People need to know that, they will come back in the future to make the choice before diverting their attention to other activities. Without this goal—when people are not told that they will make an impression or choice later—the judgments and evaluations of people who shift their minds do not differ from the RT group. Without goal guidance, the unconscious cannot think effectively.

In 2011, Dijksterhuis systematically reviewed the literature and identified 92 experiments. The conclusion was that unconscious thought brings superior judgments and choices compared to reflection. Furthermore, it seems that in three situations the superiority of the unconscious thought is more obvious:

- When people have to deal with a large amount of information

- When people need to form an overall, balanced impression of all the information

- When information is presented in multiple forms, such as visual and verbal

In regards to the second point, a comprehensive understanding of all the information is important. The example of erroneous intuition we introduced in Chapter 2 that we may form two completely different impressions of the same person—when the positive characteristics come first compared to when the negative ones come first—results from insufficient attention to all the information.

For the third point, information in multiple forms needs the collaboration of different sensory systems. Perhaps it is too complex for the reflective mind to deal with.

A final, practical question. How much time should we give our unconscious thought to reach optimal decisions?

In the above experiments, the time given to the UT group was usually 2–8 minutes. But in real life, we do not have a clear timetable. Because in these experiments, people initially received accurate and comprehensive information about the options to be selected. This process in real life may take longer.

Fortunately, unconscious thought is already widely used in our daily lives. The result is often ideal. In another survey conducted outside of the entrance of a furniture center, researchers asked what people bought and how did they choose. A few weeks later, researchers contacted them again by telephone and asked them how satisfied they were with their choices.

Excluding those who did not collect any information of the product before buying, the researchers categorized people into reflective thinkers and unconscious thinkers based on how much they thought before buying. The result showed that several weeks later, the unconscious thinkers were more satisfied with their furniture than reflective thinkers.

Furniture is a complex commodity. When buying a furniture, we not only consider its price, texture, function, but also consider its color, style, and to what extent it fits with our house. This seems to be the territory of unconscious thought.

Make informed intuition

A psychologist couple once tried to use reflective thinking to buy a house. They listed all the important features of a house, including the number of rooms, the layout of the kitchen, the orientation of the windows, the height of the floors, the location, the characteristics of the neighborhood, and so on. That list was so extensive that it went on for several pages. Each time they visited a new house, they scored it for each feature on the list using a 7-grade scale: 1 very bad and 7 very good. They suspected that after doing so, it would be easy to quantify their preferences and they could finally make the optimal choice.

However, after scoring several houses, they found themselves more confused, and unsure of what house they liked. They said something like this: "We ended up throwing away that list and turned to our intuition to determine which house we liked the best." In the end, they bought a house they absolutely loved and have lived there happily for decades.

Psychologist Timothy D. Wilson calls the wise intuition "informed intuition" and argues that, "we need to gather as much information as possible, which allows us to make a steady, informed assessment of our adaptive unconsciousness."

We have sufficient knowledge in our long-term memory about our preferences. Personal preference is an ordinary person's expert intuition. So as the next step, we just need to collect accurate, comprehensive, and representative information about our options to make the ideal choice. From this point of view, the extensive list created by the above psychologist couple was helpful: it assisted them in getting a complete image of the house.

Finally, let's get back to the decisions we make about love and marriage. Most people will not agree to marry someone immediately at first sight because we cannot get all the information in such a short amount of time. If after we go out with someone for a longer period of time, collect enough information, and become familiar with each other, we still love each other, then this is an informed intuition we can trust.

In this process, the work of the conscious and reflective mind is to gather enough information, and the work of the unconscious is to integrate that information and tell us the conclusion: an informed intuition. And we should trust this intuition even if it is not reasonably justifiable.

Chapter 5. Educate Your Intuition in Everyday Life

The greatest obstacle to discovery was not ignorance but the illusion of knowledge.

— Daniel J. Boorstin,
The Discoverers: A History of Man's Search to Know His World and Himself (1983)

To cultivate accurate intuition, we must accumulate enough knowledge in our long-term memory. As we have seen, expert intuition is the best intuition. But expert intuition is domain-specific. Training and learning in one area does not transfer to another and guarantee similarly professional judgments. It is impossible to develop expert intuition in every field, yet, what we can do is learn like an expert.

We must appreciate every decision we make as a learning opportunity and keep improving the accuracy of our intuition. Each time, after deciding and experiencing its outcome, we obtain timely and effective feedback to update our knowledge and accumulate new associations (cue-outcome). This is essentially a trial-and-error approach to learning. Whereas positive feedback reinforces the decision (cue-outcome association), negative ones weaken it.

Unfortunately, this approach has severe problems. In everyday life, while people can get accurate and timely feedback on decisions about personal preference, in many other fields or with other criteria, the feedback is often of low quality.

Suboptimal feedback that hinders learning

You can choose among three pieces of chocolate: dark, milk, and white. After tasting each, you find you prefer milk chocolate. Dark is too bitter and white too sweet. Milk chocolate is well-balanced. This is a typical example of the learning experience. Dark, milk, and white chocolates are the cues, and their respective taste is the outcome. Your choice as judged by taste is perfect.

But taste is merely one criterion of food choice. Health, for example, is another, although many people tend to ignore or be unaware of this criterion. Therein lies the problem. We seldom experience the health consequences of our food choices immediately and it often takes years to see the outcome. When health consequences become clear to us, it is often too late for us to take effective actions: our health has already been jeopardized and treatment is difficult.

Worse, we eat many food items each day, which makes the causal attribution of the consequence to specific food items difficult, if based on pure personal experience.

In the case of chocolate, dark has the greatest health benefit as it contains many polyphenols (antioxidant and anti-inflammatory compounds). White has hardly any polyphenols and is high in sugar (often leading to over caloric intake and impaired insulin signaling, thus a health risk). Milk chocolate is in the middle. I suspect no one would ever notice these health consequences if we solely rely on personal experience.

Another hindrance to accurate intuition in this example is that the immediate feedback of taste contradicts with the long-term feedback of health benefits. Dark tastes bitter but is healthy. This is like the old Chinese saying *liang yao ku kou* [*good medicine tastes bitter*]. At the inverse polar, things that taste good may be toxic in the long run.

When stressed, many people turn to high-fat, high-sugar foods, alcohol, or drugs for comfort. These activities can relieve their stress immediately, but will bring long-lasting damage to the mind and brain. This is like another old Chinese saying *yin zhen zhi ke* [*drinking poison to quench thirst*].

Similarly, reducing investment in developing new products and investing that money instead into marketing produces an immediate increase in profit. But that eventually leads to lack of new products and poor competitiveness. The inconsistency of the immediate with the long-term is likely to cause incorrect learning.

Without timely, accurate feedback on the health risks of food choices, our intuition on diet and related daily choices cannot be satisfactory in the long run. Similarly, our intuition on lifestyle choices, such as physical activity (physical inactivity), sleep habits (insufficient sleep or irregular sleep patterns), living environment (choice of less greenery and no-sunshine areas), marital communication (use of stonewalling), and parenting (use of corporal punishment) may also be suboptimal.

These examples cover several popular issues that compromise the quality of intuition:

- The criteria to evaluate decisions are not clear or explicitly revealed: besides pleasure, our work productivity, long-term health, and the wellbeing of our family may all be considered criteria, although they are frequently ignored;

- Feedback is late: before feedback comes, we continue to make similar decisions, the quality of which cannot be improved;

- Feedback is nonspecific: many other factors may bring similar feedback and we won't be able to create specific cue-outcome associations; in other words, no learning occurs;

- The impact of the feedback is huge: the decisions are high stakes and the price of error is high. We cannot afford to learn by personal experience;

- The immediate feedback is conflicted in the long run: this deceives our mind and causes wrong learning.

In these cases, we should use our reflective thinking to get effective feedback beforehand from other sources. In other words, we should learn from others' experiences and the findings of scientific studies. In real life, that children and adolescents tend to choose food primarily based on their preference of taste while older individuals balance both taste and health value is an illustration. As we grow older, we gradually realize the importance of health and get feedback (either personal or that of others) on the health impacts of food on our lives.

The fundamental limitation of intuition: no trial, no learning

The learning rule of intuition is trial-and-error. That means, no trial, no learning. If we have no chance of trying a certain choice, we won't get feedback on it, least of all learning anything. When stressed, if you always eat junk food and drink alcohol to seek comfort, and never try physical exercise and meditation, how would you know the latter is actually more effective unless you have been told?

Meanwhile, the operational rule of intuition is association. This may sometimes constrain learning. For instance, our immediate reaction to the message that wine promotes health is to drink more wine, as the cue in this association is wine. However, drinking more wine is not the optimal decision because wine is not the fundamental cue that accounts for its outcome health benefits. The ultimate cue here is polyphenols contained in wine. Therefore, the rational choice here is to consume more foods rich in polyphenols, such as green tea, berries, and nuts (e.g., walnuts). This reminds us of the importance of using the reflective mind to identify the correct cue, not fake ones.

Use reflection to train intuition

The good news is that we can use our reflective mind to create a good learning environment and educate our intuition. The first step towards better intuition and decision-making is to specify our value system, namely what is important to us, what our motives and goals are. The value system is the criteria for evaluating all our decisions in everyday life. The criteria we often ignore are our health (physical and mental), work productivity, and the wellbeing of our family. Many people think they care about these things, but their behavior suggests otherwise.

As the second step, each time we decide, we collect as much information as possible about our options.

For the third step, after each decision, seek timely, accurate, representative feedback as evaluated by the above criteria, namely our value system.

If the choices presented to us are high stakes, or the feedback is late, nonspecific, or non-representative, try to learn from others' experiences and scientific findings, and use that knowledge as feedback to adjust your daily behavior and decisions. This will provide you shortcuts and save you lots of pain.

I have selected and written a number of scientific books and resources most relevant to our decision-making in everyday life and put them on brainandlife.net. Check and see how it helps you from now.

The end

This is the whole tale of the two minds. I hope the tale has given you fresh eyes and helps you reconsider your everyday choices. Intuition is quick and efficient in guiding our daily activities. It is also the key to making tough, important life decisions because it "knows" our values, or our "heart." The common conflict people often run into, that is, between listening to our heart and following our head, is resolved.

Both the heart and head have a role to play in making decisions. What we can do is to get familiar with each one's strengths and weaknesses and in what situation each prevails. Although in this book, we devoted most of our focus on how to achieve accurate, expert intuition, it is equally important to optimize the reflective mind.

Best of luck.

References

Preface

Special light catching cells… Dina Spector (2013 Oct. 16). *How Cats See The World Compared To Humans [PICTURES]*. Available http://www.businessinsider.com/pictures-of-how-cats-see-the-world-2013-10 (last accessed 2018-02-08); Stanley Coren (2008 Oct. 20). Can Dogs See Colors? Available https://www.psychologytoday.com/blog/canine-corner/200810/can-dogs-see-colors (last accessed 2018-02-08); Pearlman, A. L., & Daw, N. W. (1971). Behavioral and neurophysiological studies on cat color vision. *International Journal of Neuroscience*, 1(6), 357-360; Miller, P. E., & Murphy, C. J. (1995). Vision in dogs. *Journal-American Veterinary Medical Association*, 207, 1623-1634.

A devout monk… Koestler, A. (1964). *The Act of Creation*. New York: Macmillan.

Chapter 1

Iowa Gambling Task… Bechara, A., Damasio, A. R., Damasio, H., & Anderson, S. W. (1994). Insensitivity to future consequences following damage to human prefrontal cortex. *Cognition*, 50(1-3), 7-15; Bechara, A., Damasio, H., Tranel, D., & Damasio, A. R. (1997). Deciding advantageously before knowing the advantageous strategy. *Science*, 275(5304), 1293-1295; Wagar, B. M., & Dixon, M. (2006). Affective guidance in the Iowa gambling task. *Cognitive, Affective, & Behavioral Neuroscience*, 6(4), 277-290.

MIT meeting… Gardner, H. (1985). *The mind's new science: A history of the cognitive revolution.* Basic Books.

The process theory of memory… Atkinson, R. C., & Shiffrin, R. M. (1968). Human memory: A proposed system and its control processes1. In *Psychology of learning and motivation* (Vol. 2, pp. 89-195). Academic Press.

Working memory… Velichkovsky, B. B. (2017). Consciousness and working memory: Current trends and research perspectives. *Consciousness and cognition*, 55, 35-45.

Unconsciousness… Tamietto, M., & de Gelder, B. (2010). Neural bases of the non-conscious perception of emotional signals. *Nature Reviews Neuroscience*, 11, 697-709; Kandel, E. (2012). *The Age of Insight: The Quest to Understand the Unconscious in Art, Mind, and Brain, from Vienna1900 to the Present.* Random House.

Adaptive unconscious… Wilson, T.D. (2002). *Strangers to ourselves: discovering the adaptive unconscious.* Cambridge, Mass.: Belknap Press of Harvard University Press.

Two modes of thinking… Epstein, S. (2012). Cognitive-experiential self-theory: An integrative theory of personality. In H. Tennen & J. Suls (Eds.). *Handbook of Psychology, 2ed., Vol.5. Personality Section.* Hoboken, NJ: John Wiley & Sons; Epstein, S. (1990). Cognitive-experiential Self-theory. In L.

References

Pervin (Ed.), *Handbook of personality theory and research: Theory and research* (pp. 165-192). NY: Guilford Publications, Inc.; Mischel, W. & Shoda, Y. (1995). A cognitive-affective system theory of personality: Reconceptualizing situations, dispositions, dynamics, and invariance in personality structure. *Psychological Review*, 102, 246-268; Mischel W & Ayduk O, 2011. Willpower in a cognitive affective processing system: the dynamics of delay of gratification. In K D. Vohs, R F. Baumeister (eds) *Handbook of self-regulation: research, theory, and applications (2ed)*. (pp83-105) New York, NY: Guilford Press; Chen, S., & Chaiken, S. (1999). The heuristic-systematic model in its broader context. In S. Chaiken & Y. Trope (Eds.), *Dual-process theories in social and cognitive psychology* (pp. 73-96). New York: Guilford Press.; Stanovich, K. E., & West, R. F. (2000). Individual differences in reasoning: Implications for the rationality debate? *Behavioral and Brain Sciences*, 23, 645-665.; Sloman, S. A. (1996) The empirical case for two systems of reasoning. *Psychological Bulletin* 119:3-22; Hammond, K. R. (1996) *Human judgment and social policy*. Oxford University Press; Shiffrin, R. M. & Schneider, W. (1977) Controlled and automatic human information processing: II. Perceptual learning, automatic attending, and a general theory. *Psychological Review* 84:127-90.

Problem-solving... J. M. Orasanu, & T. . Connolly (1993) The reinvention of decision making, In G. A. Klein, J. Orasanu, R. Calderwood, & C. E. Zsambok (Eds.), *Decision making in action: Models and methods* (pp. 3-20). Norwood, NJ: Ablex Publishers; Kahneman, D. and A. Tversky (1979). 'Prospect

Theory: An Analysis of Decision under Risk'. *Econometrica* 47(2): 263-292; Nezu, A. M., & D'Zurilla, T. J. (2006). *Problem-solving therapy: A positive approach to clinical intervention.* Springer Publishing Company; Gardner, S. T. (2008). *Thinking your way to freedom: A guide to owning your own practical reasoning.* Temple University Press.

Weighing the pros and cons... Bell Jr., Whitfield J., ed. (1956). "Benjamin Franklin's 1772 letter to Joseph Priestley". *Mr. Franklin: A Selection from His Personal Letters.* New Haven, CT: Yale University Press.

Emotion... Lazarus, R. S. (1991). *Emotion and adaptation.* Oxford University Press on Demand.

Chapter 2

Quotation... Slovic, P., Finucane, M. L., Peters, E., & MacGregor, D. G. (2007). The affect heuristic. *European journal of operational research, 177*(3), 1333-1352.

Mental math problem... first told in Chen, C. (2017). *Fitness Powered Brains: Optimize Your Productivity, Leadership And Performance.* London: Brain & Life Publishing.

Depressive patients walk slower... Lemke, M. R., Wendorff, T., Mieth, B., Buhl, K., & Linnemann, M. (2000). Spatiotemporal gait patterns during over ground locomotion in major depression compared with healthy controls. *Journal of psychiatric research, 34*(4), 277-283.

Magic number seven... Miller, G. A. (1956). The magical number seven, plus or minus two: Some limits on our capacity for processing information. *Psychological review*, *63*(2), 81.

Conscious working memory may be only 3 to 4... Broadbent, D. E. (1975). The magic number seven after fifteen years. *Studies in long term memory*, 3-18; Cowan, N., Morey, C., & Chen, Z. (2007). The legend of the magical number seven. *Tall tales about the brain: Things we think we know about the mind, but ain't so, ed. S. Della Sala*, 45-59.

Roger N. Shepard quote... Gerd Gigerenzer, Peter M. Todd, and the ABC Research Group 1999 *Simple heuristics that make us smart*. New York ; Oxford : Oxford University Press

Story of new city... Hinton, P. R. (1993). *The psychology of interpersonal perception*. Routledge.

Harvard psychologist... Ambady, N, & Rosenthal, R. (1993). Half a minute: Predicting teacher evaluations from thin slices of nonverbal behavior and physical attractiveness. *Journal of Personality and Social Psychology*, 64, 431-441

11 million bits... Nørretranders, T. (1998). *The user illusion: Cutting consciousness down to size*. New York: Viking.

Erroneous intuition: first impression... Asch, S. E. (1946). Forming impressions of personality. *The Journal of Abnormal and Social Psychology*, 41(3), 258; Ferguson, M. J. (2007). The automaticity of evaluation. *Social psychology and the unconscious: The automaticity of higher mental processes*, 219-

64; Uleman, J. S., Adil Saribay, S., & Gonzalez, C. M. (2008). Spontaneous inferences, implicit impressions, and implicit theories. *Annu. Rev. Psychol.*, 59, 329-360.

Cognitive Reflection Test... Frederick, S. (2005). Cognitive reflection and decision making. *Journal of Economic perspectives*, 19(4), 25-42.

The "highway" of emotional response... LeDoux, J. (1998). *The emotional brain: The mysterious underpinnings of emotional life*. Simon and Schuster; Tamietto, M., & de Gelder, B. (2010). Neural bases of the non-conscious perception of emotional signals. *Nature Reviews Neuroscience*, 11, 697-709

When people see a familiar face... Gobbini MI, Haxby JV. 2006 Neural response to the visual familiarity of faces. *Brain Res Bull*. 2006, 71(1-3):76-82; Adolphs R, Tranel D, Damasio AR. 1998 The human amygdala in social judgment. *Nature*. 1998, 393(6684):470-4.

Advertisement strategy story... Wranik, T., Barrett, L., & Salovey, P. (2007). Intelligent emotion regulation: Is knowledge power? From Gross, J.(ed.) *Handbook of emotion regulation*. New York.

secondary adjustment... Koole, S. L. (2009). The psychology of emotion regulation: An integrative review. *Cognition and emotion*, 23(1), 4-41.

Phineas Gage... Harlow, J. M. (1869). *Recovery from the passage of an iron bar through the head*. D. Clapp; Macmillan,

M. (2002). *An odd kind of fame: Stories of Phineas Gage*. MIT Press.

teenagers and young adults... McRae, K., Gross, J.J., Weber, J., Robertson, E., Sokol-Hessner, P., Ray, R., Gabrieli, J., & Ochsner, K. (2012). The development of emotion regulation: An fMRI study of cognitive reappraisal in children, adolescents, and young adults. *Social Cognitive and Affective Neuroscience*, 7, 11-22; Silvers, J. A., McRae, K., Gabrieli, J. D., Gross, J. J., Remy, K. A., & Ochsner, K. N. (2012). Age-related differences in emotional reactivity, regulation, and rejection sensitivity in adolescence. *Emotion*, *12*(6), 1235.

subjects with frequent violent behaviors... Pardini DA, Phillips M. 2010 Neural responses to emotional and neutral facial expressions in chronically violent men. *J Psychiatry Neurosci.* 2010, 35(6):390-8

200,000,000 years ago... Eccles, J. C. (2012). *How the self controls its brain*. Springer Science & Business Media.

Over 80-90%... Glöckner, A. (2007). Does intuition beat fast and frugal heuristics? A systematic empirical analysis. *Intuition in judgment and decision making*, 309-325; Weber, E. U., & Lindemann, P. G. (2007). From intuition to analysis: Making decisions with our head, our heart, or by the book. *Intuition in judgment and decision making*, 191-208.

Chapter 3

thousands of couples... Gottman, J., & Silver, N. (1999). *The seven principles for making marriage work*. London: Orion Books

experienced physicians... Gladwell, M. (2007). *Blink: The power of thinking without thinking*. Back Bay Books.

Blindfolded chess... David Hooper and Kenneth Whyld 1984 *The Oxford companion to chess*. Oxford, UK ; New York: Oxford University Press

spend 5 seconds looking at... Chase, W. G., & Simon, H. A. (1973). Perception in chess. *Cognitive Psychology*, 4, 55–81.

Eye tracking... Chase, W. G., & Simon, H. A. (1973). The mind's eye in chess. In *Visual information processing* (pp. 215-281).

Even up to 15 pieces... Gobet, F., & Clarkson, G. (2004). Chunks in expert memory: Evidence for the magical number four... or is it two?. *Memory*, 12(6), 732-747.

Reduce to 6 seconds... Klein, G. A. (2017). *Sources of power: How people make decisions*. MIT press.

Long-term working memory... Ericsson, K. A., & Kintsch, W. (1995). Long-term working memory. *Psychological review*, 102(2), 211.

10,000-100,000 chunks... Simon, H. A., and K. J. Gilmartin. (1973). A simulation of memory for chess positions. *Cognitive*

Psychology 5:29-46; Gobet, F. & Simon, H. (1998). Expert chess memory: Revisiting the chunking hypothesis. *Memory*, 6, 225-255.

Think aloud method... De Groot, A. D. (1978). *Thought and choice in chess* (Vol. 4). Walter de Gruyter GmbH & Co KG; Tikhomirov, O. K., & Poznyanskaya, E. D. (1966). An investigation of visual search as a means of analyzing heuristics. *Soviet Psychology*, 5(2), 3-15; Lane, P. C., & Gobet, F. (2011). Perception in chess and beyond: Commentary on Linhares and Freitas (2010). *New Ideas in Psychology*, 29(2), 156-161.

fire chief who had over 20 years of professional experience... Klein, G. A. (2011). *Streetlights and shadows: Searching for the keys to adaptive decision making*. MIT Press.

Simon citation... Prietula, M. J., & Simon, H. A. (1989). The experts in your midst. *Harvard Business Review*, 67(1), 120-124; Simon, H. A. (1992). What is an "explanation" of behavior?. *Psychological science*, 3(3), 150-161. pp. 155.

Story of husband confession... Seligman, M. E. (2006). *Learned optimism: How to change your mind and your life*. Vintage.

When observing a couple's communication... Gottman, J., & Silver, N. (1999). *The seven principles for making marriage work*. London: Orion Books

Physicians also use recognition decisions... Feltovich, P. J., Johnson, P. E., Moller, J. H., & Swanson, D. B. (1984). LCS:

The role and development of medical knowledge in diagnostic expertise. *Readings in medical artificial intelligence*, 275-319; Coderre, S., Mandin, H. H. P. H., Harasym, P. H., & Fick, G. H. (2003). Diagnostic reasoning strategies and diagnostic success. *Medical education*, 37(8), 695-703; Barrows, H. S., Norman, G. R., Neufeld, V. R., & Feightner, J. W. (1982). The clinical reasoning of randomly selected physicians in general medical practice. Clinical and investigative medicine. *Medecine clinique et experimentale*, 5(1), 49-55; Neufeld, V. R., Norman, G. R., Feightner, J. W., & Barrows, H. S. (1981). Clinical problem-solving by medical students: A cross-sectional and longitudinal analysis. *Medical education*, 15(5), 315-322.

LCTM… Lowenstein, R. (2000). *When genius failed: the rise and fall of Long-Term Capital Management*. Random House trade paperbacks.

Greenspan… Dan Ariely (2009), The End of Rational Economics. *Harvard Business Review* http://www.nytimes.com/2008/10/24/business/economy/24panel.html?_r=0&adxnnl=1&adxnnlx=1375351426-Jc/f2PtWTVr76DsnOzmMVA (last accessed 2018/02/19)

prerequisite for accurate expert intuition… Kahneman, D., & Klein, G. (2009). Conditions for intuitive expertise: a failure to disagree. *American psychologist*, 64(6), 515.

total number of radiographs… Beam, C. A., Conant, E. F., & Sickles, E. A. (2003). Association of volume and volume-independent factors with accuracy in screening mammogram interpretation. *Journal of the National Cancer Institute*, *95*(4), 282-290; Stewart, T. R., Roebber, P. J., & Bosart, L. F. (1997). The importance of the task in analyzing expert judgment. *Organizational Behavior and Human Decision Processes*, 69, 205-219.

Chapter 4

Buyer's lies... Wilson, T.D. (2002). *Strangers to ourselves: discovering the adaptive unconscious*. Cambridge, Mass.: Belknap Press of Harvard University Press.

Speed dating... Gladwell, M. (2007). *Blink: The power of thinking without thinking*. Back Bay Books.

Romantic relationship... Wilson, T. D., Dunn, D. S., Bybee, J. A., Hyman, D. B., & Rotondo, J. A. (1984). Effects of analyzing reasons on attitude–behavior consistency. *Journal of Personality and Social Psychology*, 47(1), 5.

Painting... Wilson, T. D., Lisle, D. J., Schooler, J. W., Hodges, S. D., Klaaren, K. J., & LaFleur, S. J. (1993). Introspecting about reasons can reduce post-choice satisfaction. *Personality and Social Psychology Bulletin*, 19(3), 331-339.

patients with lesions of the ventromedial prefrontal cortex... Bechara, A. (2004). The role of emotion in decision-making: evidence from neurological patients with orbitofrontal damage. *Brain and cognition*, 55(1), 30-40.

Discussion on first impression and automatic categorization... DePaulo, B. M. (1992). Nonverbal behavior and self-presentation. *Psychological Bulletin*, 111, 203–243; Ferguson, M. J. (2007). The automaticity of evaluation. *Social psychology and the unconscious: The automaticity of higher mental processes*, 219-64; Schiller, D., Freeman, J. B., Mitchell, J. P., Uleman, J. S., & Phelps, E. A. (2009) A neural mechanism for first impressions. *Nature Neuroscience*, 12, 508-514; Ambady, N. (2010). The perils of pondering: intuition and thin slice judgements. *Psychological Inquiry*, 21, 271-278.

After graduated from Cambridge in 1831... Darwin, C. (1993). *The autobiography of Charles Darwin, 1809-1882: with original omissions restored*. WW Norton & Company.

sampling trap... Unkelbach, C., & Plessner, H. (2008). The sampling trap of intuitive judgments. *Intuition in judgment and decision making*, 283-294.

spend 1 minute analyzing why they thought the teachers... Ambady, N. & Gray, H. M. (2002). On being sad and mistaken: Mood effects on the accuracy of thin-slice judgments. *Journal of Personality and Social Psychology*, 83(4), 947-961.

University psychologist job story; house story... Wilson, T.D. (2002). *Strangers to ourselves: discovering the adaptive unconscious*. Cambridge, Mass.: Belknap Press of Harvard University Press.

in what kind of situation can reflection contribute... McMackin, J., & Slovic, P. (2000). When does explicit justification impair decision making?. *Applied Cognitive Psychology*, 14(6), 527-541.

Conscious thought... Dijksterhuis, A. (2004). Think different: The merits of unconscious thought in preference development and decision making. *Journal of Personality and Social Psychology*, 87, 586-598; Dijksterhuis, A., Bos, M. W., Nordgren, L. F., & van Baaren, R. B. (2006). On Making the Right Choice: The Deliberation-Without-Attention Effect. *Science*, 311(5763), 1005-1007; Dijksterhuis, A., & Nordgren, L.F. (2006). A Theory of Unconscious Thought. *Perspectives on Psychological Science*, 1, 95-109.

requires a goal-oriented approach... Bos MW, Dijksterhuis, A., van Baaren, R. B. (2008) On the goal-dependency of unconscious thought. *Journal of experimental social psychology*, 44, 1114-20.

systematically reviewed the literature... Strick, M., Dijksterhuis, A., Bos, M. W., van Sjoerdsma, A., & Baaren, R. B. (2011). A meta-analysis on unconscious thought effects. *Social Cognition*, 29, 738-762.

outside of the entrance of a furniture center... Dijksterhuis, A., Bos, M. W., Nordgren, L. F., & van Baaren, R. B. (2006). On Making the Right Choice: The Deliberation-Without-Attention Effect. *Science*, 311(5763), 1005-1007.

Chapter 5

Chocolate and polyphenols... Chen, C. (2018). *Chocolate and the Nobel Prize: The Book of Brain Food*. London: Brain & Life Publishing.

our intuition on other lifestyles… Chen, C. (2017). *Plato's Insight: How Physical Exercise Boosts Mental Excellence.* London: Brain & Life Publishing; Chen, C. (2017). *The Seed of Intelligence: Boost Your Baby's Developing Brain through Optimal Nutrition and Healthy Lifestyle.* London: Brain & Life Publishing; Chen, C. (2018). *Cleverland: The Science of How Nature Nurtures.* London: Brain & Life Publishing.

Index

About the Author

Dr. Chong Chen is a neuroscientist and possesses a Ph.D. in Medicine. Chong has authored 10 books, including two series called **The Anchor of Our Purest Thoughts** and **Your Baby's Developing Brain**.

As far as the future goes, Chong hopes that he will be able to translate scientific findings into ways that will allow regular people to live better lives. And through his books, he hopes that he can reach a much wider audience.

You can contact Chong and follow what he is writing about at: https://brainandlife.net